Air Fryer Cookbook For Beginners

Over 200 Flavor Filled Recipes For Beginners And Advanced Users

Lucy Miles

Table of contents

DESCRIPTION

With the growing demand for healthier cooking and better nutrition, people have turned to the air fryer as an alternative way of cooking without fat. After all, too much fat from fried foods in one's diet contributes to obesity and cardiovascular diseases. However, fat really does make food palatable. No wonder it's tough to give up that pleasant fried taste. With an air fryer, though, you capture the great taste of fried foods without the use of oil. It's a practical way for anyone striving to become slim and healthy. Healthy food should not be a fad or an impossibility to choose; it should be part of everyone's life. Of course, this does not mean that you must give up enjoying the kitchen; neither of the many dishes that can be prepared healthy. To get it there are certain appliances that can help you and a lot: for example, an air fryer. The concept of an air fryer is to fry food items in the air instead of oil. This revolutionary kitchen appliance uses superheated air that circulates to cook the food. This way, you don't have to dunk your food in sizzling hot fat just to achieve that crunch. Regarding structure, an air fryer almost looks like a large rice cooker but with a front door handle. It has a removable chunky tray that holds the food to the air fried. It has an integrated timer to allow you to pre- set cooking times, and an adjustable temperature control so you can pre-set the best cooking temperature.

Different models offer different features, such as digital displays, auto-power shut-off, but mostly they work the same and use the same technology.

Having an air fryer is a great option. You can enjoy a healthier meal and save a good part of the oil expense, all without giving up enjoyable, fried foods. This book covers the following topics:

- *Breakfast*
- *Mains*
- *Sides*
- *Seafood*
- *Poultry*
- *Meat*
- *Vegetables*
- *Soups and stews*
- *Snacks*
- *Desserts and more!!!*

INTRODUCION

Air fryers are designed to be super easy to use. Here's a little guide to get you started.

Choose a recipe

Choose a recipe that you can cook in your air fryer. Remember that most foods that you cook in your microwave or oven, or on the stovetop, can be prepared in the air fryer – except for those recipes that have a lot of fat or liquids. You can use my air fryer cookbook to help you find suitable recipes.

Prepare the air fryer

Read through the recipe to the end, so you know what accessories you need for cooking. Some recipes call for using the basket, rack, or rotisserie that comes with the air fryer. Other recipes use cake or muffin pans that you can insert into the air fryer. Just be sure these pans fit into the fryer and are safe to use.

Prepare the ingredients

Gather the ingredients for the recipe and prep them according to the instructions. When prepped, put the ingredients into the air fryer or in the basket, rack, or pans within the air fryer. Use parchment baking paper or a light mist of oil spray to prevent food from sticking.

Never crowd food in the air fryer or over-fill. Food that is crowded in the air fryer won't cook evenly and can be raw and under-cooked. If you're preparing for a crowd, you may have to cook more than one batch.

Setting the temperature and time

Check the recipe for the correct temperature and time setting. You can set manually, or you can use the digital setting for the temperature and time needed for the recipe. Most air fryers also have preset functions that make it easy to set according to each recipe.

Check food during cooking

Many air fryer recipes require you to check the food while it's cooking so that it cooks evenly and doesn't over-cook. All you need to do is shake, flip, or toss the food to distribute it. Or for some recipes, you'll need to turn the food about halfway through when cooking so that it cooks and crisps thoroughly all the way through.

Cleaning the air fryer

Once the food is cooked, remove, and unplug the air fryer. Let it cool completely before cleaning. Follow the instructions that come with the fryer for proper cleaningr. Never scrub or use abrasive cleaners when cleaning the fryer or the fryer accessories.

BREAKFAST

1. Creamy Green Beans Bowls

Preparation time: 5 minutes

Cooking time: 20 minutes Servings: 4

INGREDIENTS

- *2 cups green beans, trimmed and halved*
- *1 cup heavy cream*
- *2 eggs, whisked*
- *1 tablespoon chives, chopped*
- *½ teaspoon sweet paprika*
- *Salt and black pepper to the taste*
- *1 teaspoon hot paprika*
- *1 tablespoons chives, chopped*

DIRECTIONS

1. *In the air fryer's pan, combine the beans with the cream, eggs and the other ingredients, put the pan into the machine and cook at 360 degrees F for 20 minutes.*
2. *Divide the mix between plates and serve right away.*

NUTRITION:

Calories 222, Fat 11, Fiber 4, Carbs 6, Protein 12

2. Cilantro Tuna Eggs

Preparation time: 5 minutes

Cooking time: 20 minutes
Servings: 4

INGREDIENTS

- *8 eggs, whisked*
- *1 cup canned tuna, drained and flaked*
- *1 tablespoon cilantro, chopped*
- *Cooking spray*
- *1 cup mozzarella, shredded*
- *Salt and black pepper to the taste*

DIRECTIONS

1. *Grease a pan that fits your air fryer with the cooking spray, add the eggs mixed with the tuna and the other ingredients, toss, put the pan into the machine and cook at 350 degrees F for 20 minutes.*
2. *Divide between plates and serve for breakfast.*

NUTRITION: ***calories 270, fat 15, fiber 3, carbs***

5, protein 9

3. Walnuts and Berries Quinoa

Preparation time: 5 minutes

Cooking time: 20 minutes

Servings: 4

INGREDIENTS

- *¼ cup walnuts, chopped*
- *1 cup blueberries*
- *1 cup quinoa*
- *2 cups almond milk*
- *2 tablespoons sugar*

DIRECTIONS

1. *Heat up the air fryer at 350 degrees F, combine the quinoa with the walnuts and the other ingredients inside, and cook for 20 minutes.*
2. *Divide into bowls and serve for breakfast.*

NUTRITION: ***calories 216, fat 11, fiber 3, carbs***

5, protein 9

4. Quinoa and Coconut Cream Mix

Preparation time: 5 minutes

Cooking time: 20 minutes Servings: 4

INGREDIENTS

- *1 cup quinoa*
- *2 cups coconut milk*
- *½ cup coconut cream*
- *2 tablespoons walnuts, chopped*
- *1 tablespoon almonds, chopped*
- *2 tablespoon sugar*

DIRECTIONS

3. *In the air fryer, combine the quinoa with the milk, cream and the other ingredients, stir, and cook at 360 degrees F for 20 minutes.*
4. *Divide into bowls and serve for breakfast.* NUTRITION: *calories 271, fat 14, fiber 3, carbs 5, protein 11*

5. Olive Eggs

Preparation time: 5 minutes

Cooking time: 20 minutes Servings: 4

INGREDIENTS

- *½ cup black olives, pitted and sliced*
- *½ cup kalamata olives, pitted and sliced*
- *½ teaspoon chili powder*
- *8 eggs, whisked*
- *Cooking spray*
- *A pinch of salt and black pepper*

DIRECTIONS

1. *In a bowl, combine the eggs with the olives and the other ingredients except the cooking spray and whisk.*
2. *Grease a pan that fits the air fryer with the cooking spray, pour the eggs mixture inside, stir, put the pan into the machine, and cook at 360 degrees F for 20 minutes.*
3. *Divide between plates and serve for breakfast.*

NUTRITION: ***calories 220, fat 13, fiber 4, carbs***

6, protein 12

6. Swiss Chard and Avocado Mix

Preparation time: 5 minutes

Cooking time: 15 minutes Servings: 4

INGREDIENTS

- *1 cup avocado, peeled, pitted and cubed*
- *1 cup Swiss chard, torn*
- *1 teaspoon olive oil*
- *½ cup black olives, pitted and sliced*
- *4 eggs, whisked*
- *1 cup tomatoes, cubed*
- *Salt and black pepper to the taste*

DIRECTIONS

5. *In a bowl, mix the avocado with the chard and the other ingredients except the oil and stir well.*
6. *Grease a pan that fits the fryer with the oil, pour the mix and cook at 359 degrees F for 15 minutes.*
7. *Divide between plates and serve for breakfast.*

NUTRITION: ***calories 202, fat 14, fiber 3, carbs***

5, protein 12

7. Salmon Salad

Preparation time: 5 minutes

Cooking time: 20 minutes Servings: 4

INGREDIENTS

- *Cooking spray*
- *1 pound salmon fillets, boneless and cubed*
- *1 cup baby kale*
- *1 cup cherry tomatoes, halved*
- *4 scallions, chopped*
- *A pinch of salt and black pepper*
- *1 cup black olives, pitted and halved*

DIRECTIONS

8. *Grease the Air Fryer with the oil, preheat it at 360 degrees F, add the salmon and the scallions and cook for 5 minutes.*
9. *Add the rest of the ingredients, toss, cook for 15 minutes more, divide between plates and serve for breakfast.*

NUTRITION: ***calories 230, fat 12, fiber 3, carbs***

5,
protein 12

8. Mushroom and Onion Spread

Preparation time: 5 minutes

Cooking time: 20 minutes Servings: 4

INGREDIENTS

- *1 cup white mushrooms*
- *1 cup yellow onion, chopped*
- *2 tablespoons tahini paste*
- *Juice of 1 lime*
- *½ cup heavy cream*
- *A pinch of salt and black pepper*
- *Cooking spray*

DIRECTIONS

10. *Put the mushrooms in your air fryer's basket, grease with cooking spray, season with salt and pepper and cook at 360 degrees F for 20 minutes.*
11. *Transfer to a blender, add the onion, tahini paste and the remaining ingredients, pulse well, divide into bowls and serve as a morning spread.*

NUTRITION: ***calories 202, fat 12, fiber 2,***

carbs 5, protein 7

9. Shrimp and Spring Onions Salad

Preparation time: 5 minutes

Cooking time: 15 minutes Servings: 4

INGREDIENTS

- *1 pound shrimp, peeled and deveined*
    - *1 cup baby spinach*
    - *½ cup spring onions, chopped*
    - *Juice of 1 lime*
    - *1 cup cherry tomatoes, halved*
    - *1 tablespoon olive oil*
    - *A pinch of salt and black pepper*

DIRECTIONS

12. *Preheat the Air Fryer with the oil over 360 degrees F, add the shrimp, spinach and the other ingredients, toss, cook for 15 minutes, divide into bowls and serve for breakfast.*

NUTRITION: ***calories 212, fat 8, fiber 3, carbs***

5, protein 8

10. Minty Shrimp and Eggs

Preparation time: 5 minutes

Cooking time: 15 minutes Servings: 4

INGREDIENTS

- *1 tablespoon avocado oil*
- *1 cup shrimp, peeled, deveined and chopped*
- *6 eggs, whisked*
- *½ cup heavy cream*
- *1 tablespoon mint, chopped*
- *Salt and black pepper to the taste*

DIRECTIONS

In a bowl, combine the shrimp with the eggs and the other ingredients except the oil and whisk. Heat up the air fryer with the oil at 360 degrees F, add the shrimp and eggs mix, cook for 15 minutes, divide between plates and serve.

NUTRITION: ***calories 212, fat 9, fiber 4, carbs***

5, protein 11

11. Walnuts Oatmeal

Preparation time: 5 minutes

Cooking time: 15 minutes Servings: 4

INGREDIENTS

- *1 cup walnuts, chopped*
- *1 cup coconut cream*
- *½ cup old fashioned oats*
- *1 cup almond milk*
- *2 tablespoons sugar*
- *1 teaspoon vanilla extract*

DIRECTIONS

13. *In the air fryer's pan, combine the cream with the walnuts and the other ingredients, toss and cook at 360 degrees F for 15 minutes.*
14. *Divide into bowls and serve for breakfast.* NUTRITION: *calories 201, fat 13, fiber 2, carbs 4, protein 7*

12. Buttery Eggs

Preparation time: 5 minutes

Cooking time: 20 minutes Servings: 4

INGREDIENTS

- *8 eggs, whisked*
- *2 tablespoons butter, melted*
- *½ teaspoon turmeric powder*
- *½ teaspoon chili powder*
- *A pinch of salt and black pepper*

DIRECTIONS

1. Heat up the air fryer at 350 degrees F, add the melted butter and the other ingredients, toss well, cook for 20 minutes, divide the mix between plates and serve.

NUTRITION: *calories 220, fat 12, fiber 4, carbs*

5,
protein 8

13. Stevia Rice Pudding

Preparation time: 5 minutes Cooking time: 20 minutes
Servings: 4

- *1 cup white rice*
- *2 cups coconut milk*
- *2 tablespoons stevia*
- *½ teaspoon vanilla extract*

DIRECTIONS

In a pan that fits the air fryer, combine the rice with the milk and whisk well. Introduce the in your air fryer, cook at 360 degrees F for 20 minutes, divide into bowls and serve for breakfast.

NUTRITION: ***calories 211, fat 11, fiber 3, carbs***

4, protein 8

14. Mozzarella Shrimp Mix

Preparation time: 5 minutes Cooking time: 15 minutes Servings: 4

INGREDIENTS

- *1 pound shrimp, peeled and deveined*
- *1 cup mozzarella, shredded*
- *6 eggs, whisked*
- *2 green onions, sliced*
- *1 tablespoon olive oil*
- *A pinch of salt and black pepper*

DIRECTIONS

1. *In a bowl, mix all the ingredients except the oil and whisk.*
2. *Preheat the air fryer with the oil at 360 degrees F, add the shrimp mix, spread and cook for 15 minutes, shaking the fryer once.*
3. *Divide the mix between plates and serve for breakfast.*
4. *NUTRITION: calories 222, fat 12, fiber 4, carbs 5, protein 7*

15. Sage Scramble

Preparation time: 5 minutes

Cooking time: 20 minutes Servings: 4

INGREDIENTS

- *8 eggs, whisked*
- *2 tablespoons sage, chopped*
- *½ cup heavy cream*
- *Salt and black pepper to the taste*
- *½ teaspoon turmeric powder*
- *½ teaspoon garam masala*

DIRECTIONS

Heat up the air fryer at 350 degrees F, add the eggs mixed with the sage, cream and the other ingredients, toss and cook for 20 minutes.

Divide the mix between plates and serve for breakfast.

NUTRITION: calories 221, fat 12, fiber 4, carbs 5, protein 9

16. Tomato, Avocado and Watercress Salad

Preparation time: 4 minutes

Cooking time: 15 minutes
Servings: 4

INGREDIENTS

- *1 cup watercress, torn*
- *1 cup avocado, peeled, pitted and roughly cubed*
- *1 cup cherry tomatoes, halved*
- *Juice of 1 lime*
- *1 tablespoon olive oil*
- *Cooking spray*

DIRECTIONS

Grease a pan that fits the air fryer with the cooking spray, add the avocado, tomatoes and the other ingredients, toss and cook at 360 degrees F for 15 minutes.
Divide into bowls and serve for breakfast.

NUTRITION: ***calories 202, fat 11, fiber 3, carbs***

5,
protein 4

17. Herbed Sprouts Eggs

Preparation time: 5 minutes

Cooking time: 15 minutes Servings: 4

INGREDIENTS

- *1 tablespoon olive oil*
- *1 cup green onions, chopped*
- *1 cup Brussels sprouts, trimmed and halved*
- *8 eggs, whisked*
- *2 cups mustard greens*
- *A pinch of salt and black pepper*
- *1 tablespoon chives, chopped*

1. *Heat up your air fryer with the oil at 360 degrees F, add the onions, sprouts and the other ingredients, toss, cook for 15 minutes shaking halfway, divide between plates and serve for breakfast.*

NUTRITION: ***Calories 224, Fat 8, Fiber 2,***

Carbs 3,
Protein 7

18. Radish and Avocado Bowls

Preparation time: 5 minutes

Cooking time: 15 minutes Servings: 4

INGREDIENTS

- *2 cups radishes, sliced*
- *1 cup avocado, peeled, pitted and cubed*
- *1 tablespoon olive oil*
- *2 eggs, whisked*
- *A pinch of salt and blackpepper*
- *1 tablespoon chives, chopped*

DIRECTIONS

1. *Grease a pan that fits the air fryer with the oil, add the radishes, avocado and all the other ingredients, toss and cook at 360 degrees F for 15 minutes.*
2. *Divide into bowls and serve for breakfast.* NUTRITION: *Calories 212, Fat 12, Fiber 3, Carbs 4, Protein 9*

19. Broccoli Rice Bowls

Preparation time: 5 minutes

Cooking time: 20 minutes Servings: 4

- *1 cup wild rice*
- *1 cup veggie stock*
- *1 cup broccoli florets*
- *1 tablespoon olive oil*
- *Juice of 1 lime*
- *A pinch of salt and black pepper*
- *1 teaspoon chili powder*
- *2 eggs, whisked*

DIRECTIONS

1. *In your air fryer, combine the rice with the stock, broccoli and the other ingredients, toss, cook at 370 degrees F for 20 minutes, shaking halfway, divide into bowls and serve for breakfast.*

NUTRITION: Calories 219, Fat 14, Fiber 3, Carbs
5, Protein 7

20. Carrots, Eggs and Radish Bowls

Preparation time: 5 minutes

Cooking time: 15 minutes Servings: 4

INGREDIENTS

- *1 cup carrots, peeled and cubed*
- *1 cup radishes, halved*
- *4 eggs, whisked*
- *1 tablespoon avocado oil*
- *1 red onion, chopped*
- *1 avocado, peeled, pitted and cubed*
- *Salt and black pepper to the taste*

DIRECTIONS

1. *Grease your air fryer with the oil, combine the radishes with the carrots, eggs and the other ingredients inside, toss, cover and cook at 370 degrees F for 15 minutes.*
2. *Divide into bowls and serve for breakfast.*

NUTRITION: Calories 209, Fat 8, Fiber 2,
Carbs 4,

Protein 9

21. Mozzarella Peppers, Avocado and Egg Bake

Preparation time: 5 minutes

Cooking time: 20 minutes Servings: 4

INGREDIENTS

- *1 tablespoon olive oil*
- *½ cup orange bell peppers, chopped*
- *4 eggs, whisked*
- *1 cup avocado, peeled, pitted and cubed*
- *½ cup red bell pepper, chopped*
- *Salt and black pepper to the taste*
- *1 teaspoon garam masala*
- *1 cup mozzarella, shredded*

DIRECTIONS

1. *Preheat the Air Fryer with the oil at 350 degrees F, add the peppers, eggs and the other ingredients, toss and cook for 20 minutes.*
2. *Divide between plates and serve for breakfast.*

NUTRITION: ***Calories 230, Fat 11, Fiber 2, Carbs***

4, Protein 6

22. Cinnamon Pears Rice

Preparation time: 4 minutes

Cooking time: 20 minutes Servings: 2

INGREDIENTS

- *½ teaspoon cinnamon powder*
- *1 cup white rice*
- *1 cup pears, peeled and cubed*
- *2 cups almond milk*
- *2 tablespoons heavy cream*

DIRECTIONS

1. *In the Air Fryer, combine the rice with the cinnamon and the other ingredients, toss and cook at 330 degrees F for 20 minutes.*
2. *Divide into bowls and serve for breakfast.*

NUTRITION: Calories 201, Fat 11, Fiber 2, Carbs 4, Protein 6

23. Avocado and Berries Salad

Preparation time: 5 minutes

Cooking time: 8 minutes Servings: 4

INGREDIENTS

- *1 cup avocado, peeled, pitted and cubed*
- *1 cup blueberries*
- *1 cup strawberries, halved*
- *Juice of 1 lime*
- *1 cup heavy cream*
- *Cooking spray*

DIRECTIONS

1. *Grease a pan that fits your air fryer with the cooking spray, combine the avocado with the berries and the other ingredients inside, put the pan in the Air Fryer and cook at 360 degrees F for 8 minutes.*
2. *Divide the salad into bowls and serve for breakfast.*

NUTRITION: calories 220, fat 14, fiber 2,
carbs 3, protein 2

24. Zucchini Mix

Preparation time: 5 minutes

Cooking time: 20 minutes

Servings: 4

INGREDIENTS

- *1 cup zucchinis, grated*
- *1 cup mushrooms, halved*
- *6 eggs, whisked*
- *1 teaspoon turmeric powder*
- *1 teaspoon coriander, ground*
- *2 spring onions, chopped*
- *Salt and black pepper to the taste*
- *1 tablespoon olive oil*

DIRECTIONS

1. *Heat up the Air Fryer with the oil at 370 degrees F, add the zucchinis, mushrooms and the other ingredients, toss, and cook for 20 minutes.*
2. *Divide the mix between plates and serve for breakfast.*

NUTRITION: Calories 202, Fat 10, Fiber 2, Carbs 4, Protein 5

25. Artichokes and Avocado Mix .

Preparation time: 5 minutes

Cooking time: 15 minutes
Servings: 4

INGREDIENTS

- *2 cups canned artichoke hearts, drained and halved*
- *1 cup avocado, peeled, pitted and cubed*
- *Juice of 1 lime*
- *Salt and black pepper to the taste*
- *4 eggs, whisked*
- *1 green onion, chopped*
- *1 tablespoon olive oil*

DIRECTIONS

1. *Heat up the air fryer with the oil at 370 degrees F, add the artichokes, avocado and the*
2. *other ingredients, toss, cook for 15 minutes, divide between plates and serve for breakfast.*

NUTRITION: ***Calories 185, Fat 8, Fiber 2,***

Carbs 5,
Protein 8

26. Fennel Eggs Mix

Preparation time: 5 minutes

Cooking time: 20 minutes Servings: 4

INGREDIENTS

- *1 fennel bulb, shredded*
- *1 red onion, chopped*
- *8 eggs, whisked*
- *A pinch of salt and black pepper*
- *1 tablespoon olive oil*
- *Juice of 1 lime*
- *½ teaspoon coriander, ground*

DIRECTIONS

1. *Grease the air fryer's pan with the oil, and mix the fennel with the onion, eggs and the other ingredients inside.*
2. *Put the pan in the Air Fryer, cook at 370 degrees F for 20 minutes, divide between plates and serve them for breakfast.*

NUTRITION: ***Calories 200, Fat 12, Fiber 1, Carbs***

5, Protein 8

27. Avocado and Spinach Salad

Preparation time: 5 minutes

Cooking time: 10 minutes Servings: 4

INGREDIENTS

- *1 cup avocado, peeled, pitted and cubed*
- *1 cup baby spinach*
- *1 cup cherry tomatoes, halved*
- *Salt and black pepper to the taste*
- *2 tablespoons heavy cream*
- *1 tablespoon olive oil*

DIRECTIONS

1. *In your Air Fryer, combine the avocado with the spinach, tomatoes and the other ingredients, toss, cover and cook at 360 degrees F for 10 minutes.*
2. *Divide into bowls and serve for breakfast.*

NUTRITION: Calories 200, Fat 7, Fiber 3,
Carbs 4,

Protein 7

28. Cabbage, Carrots and Avocado Bowls

Preparation time: 5 minutes Cooking time: 20 minutes Servings: 4

INGREDIENTS

- *1 cup red cabbage, shredded*
- *1 cup carrots, peeled and grated*
- *1 cup avocado, peeled and cubed*
- *Juice of 1 lime*
- *2 tablespoons olive oil*
- *½ cup heavy cream*
- *Salt and black pepper to the taste*

DIRECTIONS

1. *In your Air Fryer, combine the cabbage with the avocado and the other ingredients, toss, cook at 360 degrees F for 20 minutes, divide into bowls and serve.*

NUTRITION: ***Calories 200, Fat 12, Fiber 2, Carbs***

3, Protein 8

MAINS

29. Easy Hot Dogs

Preparation time: 10 minutes

Cooking time: 7 minutes Servings: 2

INGREDIENTS

- *2 hot dog buns*
- *2 hot dogs*
- *1 tablespoon Dijon mustard*
- *2 tablespoons cheddar cheese, grated*

DIRECTIONS

1. *Put hot dogs in preheated air fryer and cook them at 390 degrees F for 5 minutes.*
2. *Divide hot dogs into hot dog buns, spread mustard and cheese, return everything to your air fryer and cook for 2 minutes more at 390 degrees F.*
3. *Serve for lunch.*
4. *Enjoy!*

NUTRITION:

Calories 211, Fat 3, Fiber 8, Carbs 12, Protein 4

30. Japanese Chicken Mix

Preparation time: 10 minutes

Cooking time: 8 minutes Servings: 2

INGREDIENTS

- *2 chicken thighs, skinless and boneless*
- *2 ginger slices, chopped*
- *3 garlic cloves, minced*
- *¼ cup soy sauce*
- *¼ cup mirin*
- *1/8 cup sake*
- *½ teaspoon sesame oil*
- *1/8 cup water*
- *2 tablespoons sugar*
- *1 tablespoon cornstarch mixed with 2 tablespoons water*
- *Sesame seeds for serving*

DIRECTIONS

1. *In a bowl, mix chicken thighs with ginger, garlic, soy sauce, mirin, sake, oil, water, sugar and cornstarch, toss well, transfer to preheated air fryer and cook at 360 degrees F for 8 minutes.*
2. *Divide among plates, sprinkle sesame seeds on top and serve with a side salad for lunch.*
3. *Enjoy!*

NUTRITION:

Calories 300, Fat 7, Fiber 9, Carbs 17, Protein 10

31. Prosciutto Sandwich

Preparation time: 10 minutes Cooking time: 5 minutes Servings: 1

INGREDIENTS

- *2 bread slices*
- *2 mozzarella slices*
- *2 tomato slices*
- *2 prosciutto slices*
- *2 basil leaves*
- *1 teaspoon olive oil*
- *A pinch of salt and black pepper*

DIRECTIONS

1. *Arrange mozzarella and prosciutto on a bread slice.*
2. *Season with salt and pepper, place in your air fryer and cook at 400 degrees F for 5 minutes.*
3. *Drizzle oil over prosciutto, add tomato and basil, cover with the other bread slice, cut sandwich in half and serve.*
4. *Enjoy!*

NUTRITION:

Calories 172, Fat 3, Fiber 7, Carbs 9,
Protein 5

32. Lentils Fritters

Preparation time: 10 minutes Cooking time: 10 minutes Servings: 2

INGREDIENTS

- *1 cup yellow lentils, soaked in water for 1 hour and drained*
- *1 hot chili pepper, chopped*
- *1 inch ginger piece, grated*
- *½ teaspoon turmeric powder*
- *1 teaspoon garam masala*
- *1 teaspoon baking powder*
  - *Salt and black pepper to the taste*
  - *2 teaspoons olive oil*
  - *1/3 cup water*
  - *½ cup cilantro, chopped*
  - *1 and ½ cup spinach, chopped*
  - *4 garlic cloves, minced*
  - *¾ cup red onion, chopped*
  - *Mint chutney for serving*

DIRECTIONS

1. *In your blender, mix lentils with chili pepper, ginger, turmeric, garam masala, baking powder, salt, pepper, olive oil, water, cilantro, spinach, onion and garlic, blend well and shape medium balls out of this mix.*
2. *Place them all in your preheated air fryer at 400 degrees F and cook for 10 minutes.*
3. *Serve your veggie fritters with a side salad for lunch.*
4. *Enjoy!*

NUTRITION:

Calories 142, Fat 2, Fiber 8, Carbs 12, Protein 4

33. Lunch Potato Salad

Preparation time: 10 minutes

Cooking time: 25 minutes Servings: 4

INGREDIENTS

- *2 pound red potatoes, halved*
- *2 tablespoons olive oil*
- *Salt and black pepper to the taste*
- *2 green onions, chopped*
- *1 red bell pepper, chopped*
- *1/3 cup lemon juice*
- *3 tablespoons mustard*

DIRECTIONS

1. *On your air fryer's basket, mix potatoes with half of the olive oil, salt and pepper and cook at 350 degrees F for 25 minutes shaking the fryer once.*
2. *In a bowl, mix onions with bell pepper and roasted potatoes and toss.*
3. *In a small bowl, mix lemon juice with the rest of the oil and mustard and whisk really well.*
4. *Add this to potato salad, toss well and serve for lunch.*
5. *Enjoy!*

NUTRITION:

Calories 211, Fat 6, Fiber 8, Carbs 12, Protein 4

34. Corn Casserole

Preparation time: 10 minutes

Cooking time: 15 minutes Servings: 4

INGREDIENTS

- *2 cups corn*
- *3 tablespoons flour*
- *1 egg*
- *¼ cup milk*
- *½ cup light cream*
- *½ cup Swiss cheese, grated*
- *2 tablespoons butter*
- *Salt and black pepper to the taste*
- *Cooking spray*

DIRECTIONS

1. *In a bowl, mix corn with flour, egg, milk, light cream, cheese, salt, pepper and butter and stir well.*
2. *Grease your air fryer's pan with cooking spray, pour cream mix, spread and cook at 320 degrees F for 15 minutes.*
3. *Serve warm for lunch.*
4. *Enjoy!*

NUTRITION:

Calories 281, Fat 7, Fiber 8, Carbs 9, Protein 6

35. Bacon and Garlic Pizzas

Preparation time: 10 minutes

Cooking time: 10 minutes Servings: 4

INGREDIENTS

- *4 dinner rolls, frozen*
- *4 garlic cloves minced*
- *½ teaspoon oregano dried*
- *½ teaspoon garlic powder*
- *1 cup tomato sauce*
- *8 bacon slices, cooked and chopped*
- *1 and ¼ cups cheddar cheese, grated*
- *Cooking spray*

DIRECTIONS

1. *Place dinner rolls on a working surface and press them to obtain 4 ovals.*
2. *Spray each oval with cooking spray, transfer them to your air fryer and cook them at 370 degrees F for 2 minutes.*
3. *Spread tomato sauce on each oval, divide garlic, sprinkle oregano and garlic powder and top with bacon and cheese.*
4. *Return pizzas to your heated air fryer and cook them at 370 degrees F for 8 minutes more.*
5. *Serve them warm for lunch.*
6. *Enjoy!*

NUTRITION:

Calories 217, Fat 5, Fiber 8, Carbs 12, Protein 4

36. Sweet and Sour Sausage Mix

Preparation time: 10 minutes

Cooking time: 10 minutes Servings: 4

INGREDIENTS

- *1 pound sausages, sliced*
- *1 red bell pepper, cut into strips*
- *½ cup yellow onion, chopped*
- *3 tablespoons brown sugar*
- *1/3 cup ketchup*
- *2 tablespoons mustard*
- *2 tablespoons apple cider vinegar*
- *½ cup chicken stock*

DIRECTIONS

1. *In a bowl, mix sugar with ketchup, mustard, stock and vinegar and whisk well.*
2. *In your air fryer's pan, mix sausage slices*
3. *with bell pepper, onion and sweet and*
4. *sour mix, toss and cook at 350 degrees F for 10 minutes.*
5. *Divide into bowls and serve for lunch.*
6. *Enjoy!*

NUTRITION:

Calories 162, Fat 6, Fiber 9, Carbs 12, Protein 6

37. Meatballs and Tomato Sauce

Preparation time: 10 minutes

Cooking time: 15 minutes Servings: 4

INGREDIENTS

- *1 pound lean beef, ground*
- *3 green onions, chopped*
- *2 garlic cloves, minced*
- *1 egg yolk*
- *¼ cup bread crumbs*
- *Salt and black pepper to the taste*
- *1 tablespoon olive oil*
- *16 ounces tomato sauce*
- *2 tablespoons mustard*

DIRECTIONS

1. *In a bowl, mix beef with onion, garlic, egg yolk, bread crumbs, salt and pepper, stir well and shape medium meatballs out of this mix.*
2. *Grease meatballs with the oil, place them in your air fryer and cook them at 400 degrees F for 10 minutes.*
3. *In a bowl, mix tomato sauce with mustard, whisk, add over meatballs, toss them and cook at 400 degrees F for 5 minutes more.*
4. *Divide meatballs and sauce on plates and serve for lunch.*
5. *Enjoy!*

NUTRITION:

Calories 300, Fat 8, Fiber 9, Carbs 16, Protein 5

38. Stuffed Meatballs

Preparation time: 10 minutes

Cooking time: 10 minutes Servings: 4

INGREDIENTS

- *1/3 cup bread crumbs*
- *3 tablespoons milk*
- *1 tablespoon ketchup*
- *1 egg*
- *½ teaspoon marjoram, dried*
- *Salt and black pepper to the taste*
- *1 pound lean beef, ground*
- *20 cheddar cheese cubes*
- *1 tablespoon olive oil*

DIRECTIONS

1. *In a bowl, mix bread crumbs with ketchup, milk, marjoram, salt, pepper and egg and whisk well.*
2. *Add beef, stir and shape 20 meatballs out of this mix.*
3. *Shape each meatball around a cheese cube, drizzle the oil over them and rub.*
4. *Place all meatballs in your preheated air fryer and cook at 390 degrees F for 10 minutes.*
5. *Serve them for lunch with a side salad.*
6. *Enjoy!*

NUTRITION:

Calories 200, Fat 5, Fiber 8, Carbs 12, Protein 5

39. Steaks and Cabbage

Preparation time: 10 minutes Cooking time: 10 minutes Servings: 4

INGREDIENTS

- *½ pound sirloin steak, cut into strips*
- *2 teaspoons cornstarch*
- *1 tablespoon peanut oil*
- *2 cups green cabbage, chopped*
- *1 yellow bell pepper, chopped*
- *2 green onions, chopped*
- *2 garlic cloves, minced*
- *Salt and black pepper to the taste*

DIRECTIONS

1. *In a bowl, mix cabbage with salt, pepper and peanut oil, toss, transfer to air fryer's basket, cook at 370 degrees F for 4 minutes and transfer to a bowl.*
2. *Add steak strips to your air fryer, also add green onions, bell pepper, garlic, salt and pepper, toss and cook for 5 minutes.*
3. *Add over cabbage, toss, divide among plates and serve for lunch.*
4. *Enjoy!*

NUTRITION:

Calories 282, Fat 6, Fiber 8, Carbs 14, Protein 6

40. Succulent Lunch Turkey Breast

Preparation time: 10 minutes Cooking time: 47 minutes Servings: 4

INGREDIENTS

- *1 big turkey breast*
- *2 teaspoons olive oil*
- *½ teaspoon smoked paprika*
- *1 teaspoon thyme, dried*
- *½ teaspoon sage, dried*
- *Salt and black pepper to the taste*
- *2 tablespoons mustard*
- *¼ cup maple syrup*
- *1 tablespoon butter, soft*

DIRECTIONS

1. *Brush turkey breast with the olive oil, season with salt, pepper, thyme, paprika and sage, rub, place in your air fryer's basket and fry at 350 degrees F for 25 minutes.*
2. *Flip turkey, cook for 10 minutes more, flip one more time and cook for another 10 minutes.*
3. *Meanwhile, heat up a pan with the butter over medium heat, add mustard and maple syrup, stir well, cook for a couple of minutes and take off heat.*
4. *Slice turkey breast, divide among plates and serve with the maple glaze drizzled on top.*
5. *Enjoy!*

NUTRITION:

Calories 280, Fat 2, Fiber 7, Carbs 16, Protein 14

41. Italian Eggplant Sandwich

Preparation time: 10 minutes

Cooking time: 16 minutes

Servings: 2

INGREDIENTS

- *1 eggplant, sliced*
- *2 teaspoons parsley, dried*
- *Salt and black pepper to the taste*
- *½ cup breadcrumbs*
- *½ teaspoon Italian seasoning*
- *½ teaspoon garlic powder*
- *½ teaspoon onion powder*
- *2 tablespoons milk*
- *4 bread slices*
- *Cooking spray*
- *½ cup mayonnaise*
- *¾ cup tomato sauce*
- *2 cups mozzarella cheese, grated*

DIRECTIONS

1. *Season eggplant slices with salt and pepper, leave aside for 10 minutes and then pat dry them well.*
2. *In a bowl, mix parsley with breadcrumbs, Italian seasoning, onion and garlic powder, salt and black pepper and stir.*
3. *In another bowl, mix milk with mayo and whisk well.*
4. *Brush eggplant slices with mayo mix, dip them in breadcrumbs, place them in your air fryer's basket, spray with cooking oil and cook them at 400 degrees F for 15 minutes, flipping them after 8 minutes.*
5. *Brush each bread slice with olive oil and arrange 2 on a working surface.*
6. *Add mozzarella and parmesan on each, add baked eggplant slices, spread tomato sauce and basil and top with the other bread slices, greased side down.*
7. *Divide sandwiches on plates, cut them in halves and serve for lunch.*
8. *Enjoy!*

NUTRITION:

Calories 324, Fat 16, Fiber 4, Carbs 39, Protein 12

42. Creamy Chicken Stew

Preparation time: 10 minutes

Cooking time: 25 minutes Servings: 4

INGREDIENTS

- *1 and ½ cups canned cream of celery soup*
- *6 chicken tenders*
- *Salt and black pepper to the taste*
- *2 potatoes, chopped*
- *1 bay leaf*
- *1 thyme spring, chopped*
- *1 tablespoon milk*
- *1 egg yolk*
- *½ cup heavy cream*

DIRECTIONS

1. *In a bowl, mix chicken with cream of celery, potatoes, heavy cream, bay leaf, thyme, salt and pepper, toss, pour into your air fryer's pan and cook at 320 degrees F for 25 minutes.*
2. *Leave your stew to cool down a bit, discard bay leaf, divide among plates and serve right away.*
3. *Enjoy!*

NUTRITION:

Calories 300, Fat 11, Fiber 2, Carbs 23, Protein 14

43. Lunch Pork and Potatoes

Preparation time: 10 minutes

Cooking time: 25 minutes

Servings: 2

INGREDIENTS

- *2 pounds pork loin*
- *Salt and black pepper to the taste*
- *2 red potatoes, cut into medium wedges*
- *½ teaspoon garlic powder*
- *½ teaspoon red pepper flakes*
- *1 teaspoon parsley, dried*
- *A drizzle of balsamic vinegar*

DIRECTIONS

1. *In your air fryer's pan, mix pork with potatoes, salt, pepper, garlic powder, pepper flakes, parsley and vinegar, toss and cook at 390 degrees F for 25 minutes.*
2. *Slice pork, divide it and potatoes on plates and serve for lunch.*
3. *Enjoy!*

NUTRITION:

Calories 400, Fat 15, Fiber 7, Carbs 27, Protein 20

44. Turkey Cakes

Preparation time: 10 minutes

Cooking time: 10 minutes Servings: 4

INGREDIENTS

- *6 mushrooms, chopped*
- *1 teaspoon garlic powder*
- *1 teaspoon onion powder*
- *Salt and black pepper to the taste*
- *1 and ¼ pounds turkey meat, ground*
- *Cooking spray*
- *Tomato sauce for serving*

DIRECTIONS

1. *In your blender, mix mushrooms with salt and pepper, pulse well and transfer to a bowl.*
2. *Add turkey, onion powder, garlic powder, salt and pepper, stir and shape cakes out of this mix.*
3. *Spray them with cooking spray, transfer them to your air fryer and cook at 320 degrees F for 10 minutes.*
4. *Serve them with tomato sauce on the side and a tasty side salad.*
5. *Enjoy!*

NUTRITION:

Calories 202, Fat 6, Fiber 3, Carbs 17, Protein 10

45. Cheese Ravioli and Marinara Sauce

Preparation time: 10 minutes Cooking time: 8 minutes Servings: 6

INGREDIENTS

- *20 ounces cheese ravioli*
- *10 ounces marinara sauce*
- *1 tablespoon olive oil*
- *1 cup buttermilk*
- *2 cups bread crumbs*
- *¼ cup parmesan, grated*

DIRECTIONS

1. *Put buttermilk in a bowl and breadcrumbs in another bowl.*
2. *Dip ravioli in buttermilk, then in breadcrumbs and place them in your air fryer on a baking sheet.*
3. *Drizzle olive oil over them, cook at 400 degrees F for 5 minutes, divide them on plates, sprinkle parmesan on top and serve for lunch*
4. *Enjoy!*

NUTRITION:

Calories 270, Fat 12, Fiber 6, Carbs 30, Protein 15

46. Beef Stew

Preparation time: 10 minutes Cooking time: 20 minutes Servings: 4

INGREDIENTS

- *2 pounds beef meat, cut into medium chunks*
- *2 carrots, chopped*
- *4 potatoes, chopped*
- *Salt and black pepper to the taste*
- *1 quart veggie stock*
- *½ teaspoon smoked paprika*
- *A handful thyme, chopped*

DIRECTIONS

1. *In a dish that fits your air fryer, mix beef with carrots, potatoes, stock, salt, pepper, paprika and thyme, stir, place in air fryer's basket and cook at 375 degrees F for 20 minutes.*
2. *Divide into bowls and serve right away for lunch.*
3. *Enjoy!*

NUTRITION:

Calories 260, Fat 5, Fiber 8, Carbs 20, Protein 22

SIDES

47. Brussels Sprouts and Rhubarb Mix

Preparation time: 5 minutes

Cooking time: 20 minutes Servings: 4

INGREDIENTS

- *1 pound Brussels sprouts, trimmed and halved*
- *½ pound rhubarb, sliced*
- *2 tablespoons avocado oil*
- *Juice of 1 lemon*
- *A pinch of salt and black pepper*
- *1 tablespoon chives, chopped*
- *1 teaspoon chili paste*

DIRECTIONS

1. *In a pan that fits the air fryer, mix the sprouts with the rhubarb and the other ingredients, toss, put the pan in the fryer and cook at 390 degrees F for 20 minutes.*
2. *Divide between plates and serve as a side dish.*

NUTRITION:

Calories 200, Fat 9, Fiber 2, Carbs 6, Protein 9

48. Creamy Cauliflower

Preparation time: 5 minutes

Cooking time: 20 minutes Servings: 4

INGREDIENTS

- *1 pound cauliflower florets*
- *1 cup cream cheese, soft*
- *½ cup mozzarella, shredded*
- *½ cup coconut cream*
- *4 bacon strips, cooked and chopped*
- *Salt and black pepper to the taste*

DIRECTIONS

1. *In the air fryer's pan, mix the cauliflower with the cream cheese and the other ingredients, toss, introduce the pan in the machine and cook at 400 degrees F for 20 minutes.*
2. *Divide between plates and serve as a side dish.*

NUTRITION:

Calories 203, Fat 13, Fiber 2, Carbs 5, Protein 9

49. Cumin Cauliflower

Preparation time: 5 minutes

Cooking time: 20 minutes Servings: 4

INGREDIENTS

- *1 pound cauliflower florets*
- *1 teaspoon cumin, ground*
- *Juice of 1 lime*
- *1 tablespoon butter, melted*
- *A pinch of salt and black pepper*
- *1 tablespoon chives, chopped*
- *¼ teaspoon cloves, ground*

DIRECTIONS

1. *In the air fryer, mix the cauliflower with the cumin, lime juice and the other ingredients, toss and cook at 390 degrees F for 20 minutes.*
2. *Divide between plates and serve as a side dish.*

NUTRITION:

Calories 182, Fat 8, Fiber 2, Carbs 4, Protein 8

50. Kale Mash

Preparation time: 5 minutes

Cooking time: 20 minutes Servings: 4

INGREDIENTS

- *2 tablespoons butter, melted*
- *1 pound kale, torn*
- *1 cup heavy cream*
- *4 garlic cloves, minced*
- *2 spring onions, chopped*
- *A pinch of salt and black pepper*
- *1 tablespoon chives, chopped*

DIRECTIONS

1. *In a pan that fits the air fryer, mix the kale with the butter, cream and the other ingredients, stir, introduce the pan in the machine and cook at 380 degrees F for 20 minutes.*
2. *Blend the mix using an immersion blender, divide between plates and serve.*

NUTRITION:

Calories 198, Fat 9, Fiber 2, Carbs 6, Protein 8

51. Avocado and Cauliflower Mix

Preparation time: 5 minutes

Cooking time: 20 minutes Servings: 4

INGREDIENTS

- *2 pounds cauliflower florets*
- *1 cup avocado, peeled, pitted and cubed*
- *Juice of 1 lime*
- *½ teaspoon chili powder*
- *1 tablespoon olive oil*
- *Salt and black pepper to the taste*
- *2 garlic cloves, minced*
- *1 red chili pepper, chopped*

DIRECTIONS

1. *In a pan that fits the air fryer, mix the cauliflower with the avocado, lime juice and the other ingredients, toss, introduce the pan in the machine and cook at 380 degrees F for 20 minutes.*
2. *Divide between plates and serve as a side dish.*

NUTRITION:

Calories 187, Fat 8, Fiber 2, Carbs 5, Protein 7

52. Creamy Broccoli Quinoa

Preparation time: 5 minutes

Cooking time: 20 minutes
Servings: 4

INGREDIENTS

- *1 cup quinoa*
- *1 cup veggie stock*
- *½ cup broccoli florets*
- *2 tablespoons butter, melted*
- *1 tablespoon cilantro, chopped*
- *2 tablespoons parmesan, grated*

DIRECTIONS

1. *In a pan that fits your air fryer, mix the quinoa with the stock, broccoli and the other ingredients, stir, introduce in the fryer and cook at 360 degrees F for 20 minutes.*
2. *Divide between plates and serve as a side dish.*

NUTRITION:
Calories 193, Fat 4, Fiber 3, Carbs 5, Protein 6

53. Tomato Quinoa

Preparation time: 5 minutes Cooking time: 20 minutes Servings: 4

INGREDIENTS

- *2 tablespoons butter, melted*
- *1 cup quinoa*
- *1 cup chicken stock*
- *1 cup tomatoes, cubed*
- *1 tablespoon chives, chopped*

DIRECTIONS

1. *In the air fryer's pan, mix the quinoa with the stock and the other ingredients, toss, introduce the pan in the fryer and cook at 360 degrees F for 20 minutes.*
2. *Divide between plates and serve as a side dish.*

NUTRITION:

Calories 193, Fat 8, Fiber 2, Carbs 5,
Protein 9

54. Lemon Leeks and Broccoli

Preparation time: 5 minutes Cooking time: 20 minutes Servings: 4

INGREDIENTS

- *1 pound broccoli florets*
- *2 leeks, sliced*
- *2 tablespoons olive oil*
- *Juice of 1 lemon*
- *½ teaspoon cumin, ground*
- *½ teaspoon coriander, ground*
- *Salt and black pepper to the taste*
- *2 garlic cloves, minced*

DIRECTIONS

1. *In a pan that fits your air fryer, mix the broccoli with the leeks, oil and the other ingredients, toss, introduce the pan in the*
2. *machine and cook at 360 degrees F for 20 minutes.*
3. *Divide between plates and serve as a side dish.*

NUTRITION:

Calories 201, Fat 9, Fiber 2, Carbs 6, Protein 9

55. Balsamic Sweet Potatoes

Preparation time: 5 minutes

Cooking time: 20 minutes

Servings: 4

INGREDIENTS

- *2 pounds sweet potatoes, peeled and cut into wedges*
- *2 tablespoons balsamic vinegar*
- *2 tablespoons olive oil*
- *1 tablespoon parsley, chopped*
- *A pinch of salt and black pepper*

DIRECTIONS

1. *In the air fryer's basket, mix the sweet potatoes with the vinegar and the other ingredients, toss and cook at 400 degrees F for 20 minutes.*
2. *Divide between plates and serve as a side dish.*

NUTRITION:

Calories 203, Fat 9, Fiber 3, Carbs 6,
Protein 5

56. Creamy Zucchini Noodles

Preparation time: 5 minutes

Cooking time: 15 minutes Servings: 4

INGREDIENTS

- *1 pound zucchinis, cut with a spiralizer*
- *1 tablespoon olive oil*
- *1 cup heavy cream*
- *½ teaspoon turmeric powder*
- *1 tablespoon chives, chopped*
- *Salt and black pepper to the taste*
- *1 tablespoon basil, chopped*

DIRECTIONS

1. *In a pan that fits your air fryer, mix the zucchini noodles with the oil, cream and the other ingredients, toss, introduce in the fryer and cook at 380 degrees F for 15 minutes.*
2. *Divide between plates and serve as a side dish.*

NUTRITION:

Calories 194, Fat 7, Fiber 2, Carbs 4, Protein 9

57. Zucchini and Cucumber Mix

Preparation time: 5 minutes

Cooking time: 15 minutes Servings: 4

INGREDIENTS

- *1 pound zucchinis, roughly cubed*
- *1 cup cucumber, sliced*
- *1 cup mozzarella, shredded*
- *1 tablespoon olive oil*
- *Juice of 1 lime*
- *1 tablespoon dill, chopped*

DIRECTIONS

1. *In the air fryer's pan, mix the zucchinis with the cucumber and the other ingredients, toss, introduce in the air fryer and cook at 370 degrees F for 15 minutes.*
2. *Divide between plates and serve as a side dish.*

NUTRITION:

Calories 220, Fat 14, Fiber 2, Carbs 5, Protein 9

58. Coconut Artichokes

Preparation time: 5 minutes

Cooking time: 20 minutes Servings: 4

INGREDIENTS

- *1 tablespoon butter, melted*
- *2 cups canned artichoke hearts, drained*
- *½ cup heavy cream*
- *1 tablespoon parmesan, grated*
- *1 tablespoon dill, chopped*
- *Salt and black pepper to the taste*

DIRECTIONS

1. *In a pan that fits your air fryer, combine the artichokes with the butter, cream and the other ingredients, toss, introduce the pan in the air fryer and cook at 380 degrees F for 20 minutes.*
2. *Divide between plates and serve as a side dish.*

NUTRITION:

Calories 195, Fat 6, Fiber 2, Carbs 4, Protein 8

59. Basil Squash

Preparation time: 5 minutes

Cooking time: 20 minutes Servings: 4

INGREDIENTS

- *1 pound butternut squash, peeled and cut into wedges*
- *2 tablespoons olive oil*
- *1 tablespoon basil, chopped*
- *¼ cup lemon juice*
- *½ teaspoon sweet paprika*
- *Salt and black pepper to the taste*

DIRECTIONS

1. *In a pan that fits your air fryer, mix the squash with the oil, basil and the other ingredients, toss, introduce the pan in the air fryer and cook at 370 degrees F for 20 minutes.*
2. *Divide between plates and serve as a side dish.*

NUTRITION:

Calories 201, Fat 7, Fiber 2, Carbs 4, Protein 9

60. Pesto Sweet Potatoes

Preparation time: 5 minutes

Cooking time: 25 minutes Servings: 4

INGREDIENTS

- *1 pound sweet potatoes, peeled and cut into wedges*
- *2 tablespoons avocado oil*
- *2 tablespoons basil pesto*
- *Juice of 1 lime*
- *1 tablespoon cilantro, chopped*
- *Salt and black pepper to the taste*

DIRECTIONS

1. *In the air fryer's basket, combine the sweet potatoes with the oil, pesto and the other ingredients, toss and cook at 370 degrees F for 25 minutes.*
2. *Divide between plates and serve as a side dish.*

NUTRITION:

Calories 200, Fat 8, Fiber 2, Carbs 4, Protein 10

61. Cheddar Green Beans

Preparation time: 5 minutes

Cooking time: 20 minutes Servings: 4

INGREDIENTS

- *2 pounds green beans, trimmed and halved*
- *1 cup cheddar cheese, shredded*
- *1 cup heavy cream*
- *2 teaspoons turmeric powder*
- *1 teaspoon turmeric powder*
- *A pinch of salt and black pepper*

DIRECTIONS

1. *In the air fryer's pan, mix the green beans with the cheese, cream and the other ingredients, toss, put the pan in the machine and cook at 370 degrees F for 20 minutes.*
2. *Divide between plates and serve as a side dish.*

NUTRITION:

Calories 120, Fat 5, Fiber 1, Carbs 4, Protein 2

62. Asparagus and Pineapple Mix

Preparation time: 5 minutes

Cooking time: 20 minutes Servings: 4

INGREDIENTS

- *1 pound asparagus stalks*
- *1 cup pineapple, peeled and cubed*
- *2 tablespoons avocado oil*
- *1 tablespoon balsamic vinegar*
- *Salt and black pepper to the taste*
- *1 teaspoon sweet paprika*

DIRECTIONS

1. *In the air fryer's pan, mix the asparagus with the pineapple, oil and the other ingredients, toss, put the pan in the machine and cook at 370 degrees F for 20 minutes.*
2. *Divide between plates and serve.*

NUTRITION:

Calories 187, Fat 6, Fiber 2, Carbs 4, Protein 9

63. Garlic Sprouts

Preparation time: 5 minutes

Cooking time: 20 minutes Servings: 4

INGREDIENTS

- *1 pound Brussels sprouts, trimmed and halved*
- *3 garlic cloves, minced*
- *1 tablespoon avocado oil*
- *Salt and black pepper to the taste*
- *Juice of ½ lemon*

DIRECTIONS

1. *In the air fryer's pan, mix the sprouts with the garlic, oil and the other ingredients, toss, put the pan in the machine and cook at 400 degrees F for 20 minutes.*
2. *Divide between plates and serve.*

NUTRITION:

Calories 173, Fat 12, Fiber 2, Carbs 5, Protein 7

64. Mustard Greens and Corn Mix

Preparation time: 5 minutes

Cooking time: 15 minutes Servings: 4

INGREDIENTS

- *1 pound mustard greens*
- *1 cup corn*
- *1 tablespoon olive oil*
- *1 tablespoon balsamic vinegar*
- *A pinch of salt and black pepper*
- *1 tablespoon chives, chopped*

DIRECTIONS

1. *In a pan that fits your air fryer, mix the mustard greens with the corn, oil and the other ingredients, toss, introduce in the air fryer and cook at 360 degrees F for 15 minutes.*
2. *Divide between plates and serve as a side dish.*

NUTRITION:

Calories 121, Fat 3, Fiber 4, Carbs 6, Protein 5

65. Hot Zucchini Rice

Preparation time: 5 minutes

Cooking time: 20 minutes Servings: 4

INGREDIENTS

- *1 cup wild rice*
- *2 cups veggie stock*
- *½ cup zucchinis, cubed*
- *1 red onion, chopped*
- *½ teaspoon chili powder*
- *2 teaspoons olive oil*
- *Salt and black pepper to the taste*
- *¼ cup parsley, chopped*

DIRECTIONS

1. *In a pan that fits your air fryer, combine the rice with the stock, zucchinis and the other ingredients, introduce in the fryer and cook at 370 degrees F for 20 minutes.*
2. *Divide between plates and serve as a side dish.*

NUTRITION:

Calories 200, Fat 6, Fiber 3, Carbs 4,
Protein 5

66. Parsley Zucchini and Radishes

Preparation time: 5 minutes

Cooking time: 15 minutes Servings: 4

INGREDIENTS

- *1 pound zucchinis, cubed*
- *1 cup radishes, halved*
- *1 tablespoon olive oil*
- *1 tablespoon balsamic vinegar*
- *2 tomatoes, cubed*
- *3 tablespoons parsley, chopped*
- *Salt and black pepper to the taste*

DIRECTIONS

1. *In a pan that fits your air fryer, mix the zucchinis with the radishes, oil and the other ingredients, toss, introduce in the fryer and cook at 350 degrees F for 15 minutes.*
2. *Divide between plates and serve as a side dish.*

NUTRITION:

Calories 170, Fat 6, Fiber 2, Carbs 5, Protein 6

67. Cherry Tomatoes Sauté

Preparation time: 5 minutes Cooking time: 15 minutes Servings: 4

INGREDIENTS

- *1 tablespoon olive oil*
- *1 pound cherry tomatoes, halved*
- *Juice of 1 lime*
- *2 tablespoons parsley, chopped*
- *A pinch of salt and blackpepper*

DIRECTIONS

1. *In a pan that fits the air fryer, mix the tomatoes with the oil and the other ingredients, toss, introduce the pan in the machine and cook at 360 degrees F for 15 minutes.*
2. *Divide between plates and serve.*

NUTRITION:

Calories 141, Fat 6, Fiber 2, Carbs 4, Protein 7

68. Creamy Eggplant

Preparation time: 5 minutes

Cooking time: 20 minutes Servings: 4

INGREDIENTS

- *2 pounds eggplants, roughly cubed*
- *1 cup heavy cream*
- *2 tablespoons butter, melted*
- *Salt and black pepper to the taste*
- *½ teaspoon chili powder*
- *½ teaspoon turmeric powder*

DIRECTIONS

1. *In a pan that fits the air fryer, mix the eggplants with the cream, butter and the other ingredients, toss, introduce in the machine and cook at 370 degrees F for 20 minutes.*
2. *Divide between plates and serve as a side dish.*

NUTRITION:

Calories 151, Fat 3, Fiber 2, Carbs 4, Protein 6

SEAFOOD

69. Maple Dijon Baked Salmon

Preparation time: 5 minutes

Cooking time: 18 minutes Servings: 5

INGREDIENTS

- *1 ½ pounds salmon*
- *¼ cup parsley, freshly chopped*
- *¼ cup Dijon mustard*
- *1 Tbsp olive oil*
- *1 tsp maple extract*
- *1 Tbsp fresh squeezed lemon juice*
- *1 Tbsp minced garlic*
- *¼ tsp salt*
- *¼ tsp ground black pepper*

DIRECTIONS

1. *Preheat your air fryer to 375 degrees F line your air fryer tray with a piece of parchment paper.*
2. *Place the salmon on the parchment lined tray.*
3. *In a small bowl, mix together the remaining ingredients and then spread over the top of the salmon.*
4. *Place the salmon in the air fryer and bake for 18 minutes. Slice and serve hot!*

NUTRITION:

Calories 254, Total Fat 13g, Saturated Fat 2g, Total Carbs 2g, Net Carbs 1g, Protein 31g, Sugar 0g, Fiber 1g, Sodium 373mg, Potassium 42g

70. Creamy Baked Scallops

Preparation time: 5 minutes

Cooking time: 5 minutes Servings: 4

INGREDIENTS

- *1 pound jumbo scallops*
- *1 Tbsp butter*
- *1 Tbsp heavy cream*
- *¼ tsp salt*
- *¼ tsp ground blackpepper*

DIRECTIONS

1. *Preheat your air fryer to 400 degrees F and line your air fryer tray with foil.*
2. *Place the butter on the air fryer tray and place inside the air fryer for one minute to melt.*
3. *Remove the tray and add the scallops, heavy cream, and seasonings, toss together and return to the air fryer for 5 minutes. The bottom of the scallops should be golden brown.*
4. *Serve hot.*

NUTRITION:

Calories 174, Total Fat 10g, Saturated Fat 45g, Total Carbs 3g, Net Carbs 2g, Protein 13g, Sugar 0g, Fiber 1g, Sodium 644mg, Potassium 232g

71. Cajun Seared Scallops

Preparation time: 5 minutes

Cooking time: 5 minutes Servings: 4

INGREDIENTS

- *1 pound jumbo scallops*
- *2 Tbsp butter*
- *½ tsp Cajun seasoning*

DIRECTIONS

1. *Preheat your air fryer to 400 degrees F and line your air fryer tray with foil.*
2. *Place the butter on the air fryer tray and place inside the air fryer for one minute to melt.*
3. *Remove the tray and add the scallops and seasonings, toss together and return to the air fryer for 5 minutes. The bottom of the scallops should be golden brown.*
4. *Serve hot.*

NUTRITION:

Calories 161, Total Fat 9g, Saturated Fat 4g, Total Carbs 3g, Net Carbs 2g, Protein 13g, Sugar 0g, Fiber 1g, Sodium 627mg, Potassium 230g

72. Crispy Scallops

Preparation time: 5 minutes

Cooking time: 5 minutes Servings: 4

INGREDIENTS

- *1 pound jumbo scallops*
- *2 Tbsp butter*
- *¼ tsp salt*
- *¼ tsp ground black pepper*
- *¼ cup ground pork rinds*

DIRECTIONS

1. *Preheat your air fryer to 400 degrees F and line your air fryer tray with foil.*
2. *Place the butter on the air fryer tray and place inside the air fryer for one minute to melt.*
3. *Remove the tray and add the scallops, pork rinds, and seasonings, toss together and return to the air fryer for 5 minutes. The bottom of the scallops should be golden brown.*
4. *Serve hot.*

NUTRITION:

Calories 182, Total Fat 11g, Saturated Fat 6g, Total Carbs 3g, Net Carbs 2g, Protein 13g, Sugar 0g, Fiber 1g, Sodium 647mg, Potassium 241g

73. Bacon Scallops

Preparation time: 5 minutes

Cooking time: 5 minutes Servings: 4

INGREDIENTS

- *1 pound jumbo scallops*
- *1 Tbsp butter*
- *¼ cup cooked, crumbled bacon*
- *¼ tsp salt*
- *¼ tsp ground black pepper*

DIRECTIONS

1. *Preheat your air fryer to 400 degrees F and line your air fryer tray with foil.*
2. *Place the butter on the air fryer tray and place inside the air fryer for one minute to melt.*
3. *Remove the tray and add the scallops, bacon and seasonings, toss together and return to the air fryer for 5 minutes. The bottom of the scallops should be golden brown.*
4. *Serve hot.*

NUTRITION:

Calories 189, Total Fat 12g, Saturated Fat 6g, Total Carbs 3g, Net Carbs 2g, Protein 13g, Sugar 0g, Fiber 1g, Sodium 640mg, Potassium 232g

74. Scallops and Spinach

Preparation time: 5 minutes

Cooking time: 5 minutes Servings: 4

INGREDIENTS

- *1 pound jumbo scallops*
- *3 cups baby spinach*
- *2 Tbsp butter*
- *¼ tsp salt*
- *¼ tsp ground black pepper*

DIRECTIONS

1. *Preheat your air fryer to 400 degrees F and line your air fryer tray with foil.*
2. *Place the butter on the air fryer tray and place inside the air fryer for one minute to melt.*
3. *Remove the tray and add the scallops, spinach and seasonings, toss together and return to the air fryer for 5 minutes. The bottom of the scallops should be golden brown.*
4. *Serve hot.*

NUTRITION:

Calories 174, Total Fat 9g, Saturated Fat 4g, Total Carbs 5g, Net Carbs 2g, Protein 13g, Sugar 0g, Fiber 3g, Sodium 640mg, Potassium 267g

75. Salmon and Asparagus

Preparation time: 20 minutes

Cooking time: 20 minutes Servings: 5

INGREDIENTS

- *1 ¾ pound salmon fillets*
- *¼ tsp salt*
- *¼ tsp ground black pepper*
- *3 Tbsp olive oil*
- *1 pound asparagus spears*
- *1 Tbsp lemon juice*
- *1 Tbsp fresh chopped parsley*

DIRECTIONS

1. *Preheat your air fryer to 400 degrees F and line your air fryer tray with a long piece of parchment paper.*
2. *Place the salmon filets on the parchment and sprinkle with the salt and pepper and rub the spices into the fish.*
3. *Top the fish with the remaining ingredients and then wrap the parchment paper up around the fish filets, enclosing them completely.*
4. *Place the tray in the air fryer and bake for 20 minutes.*
5. *Remove from the air fryer, unwrap the parchment and serve while hot!*

NUTRITION:

Calories 257, Total Fat 10g, Saturated Fat 4g, Total Carbs 10g, Net Carbs 6g, Protein 33g, Sugar 3g, Fiber 4g, Sodium 492mg, Potassium 325g

76. Cod and Asparagus

Preparation time: 20 minutes

Cooking time: 20 minutes Servings: 5

INGREDIENTS

- *1 ¾ pound cod fillets*
- *¼ tsp salt*
- *¼ tsp ground black pepper*
- *3 Tbsp olive oil*
- *1 pound asparagus spears*
- *1 Tbsp lemon juice*
- *1 Tbsp fresh chopped parsley*

DIRECTIONS

1. *Preheat your air fryer to 400 degrees F and line your air fryer tray with a long piece of parchment paper.*
2. *Place the cod filets on the parchment and sprinkle with the salt and pepper and rub the spices into the fish.*
3. *Top the fish with the remaining ingredients and then wrap the parchment paper up around the fish filets, enclosing them completely.*
4. *Place the tray in the air fryer and bake for 20 minutes.*
5. *Remove from the air fryer, unwrap the parchment and serve while hot!*

NUTRITION:

Calories 235, Total Fat 8g, Saturated Fat 4g, Total Carbs 10g, Net Carbs 6g, Protein 33g, Sugar 3g, Fiber 4g, Sodium 492mg, Potassium 325g

77. Parmesan Salmon and Asparagus

Preparation time: 20 minutes

Cooking time: 20 minutes Servings: 5

INGREDIENTS

- *1 ¾ pound salmon fillets*
- *¼ tsp salt*
- *¼ tsp ground black pepper*
- *3 Tbsp olive oil*

- *1 pound asparagus spears*
- *½ cup grated parmesan cheese*
- *1 Tbsp lemon juice*
- *1 Tbsp fresh chopped parsley*

DIRECTIONS

1. *Preheat your air fryer to 400 degrees F and line your air fryer tray with a long piece of parchment paper.*
2. *Place the salmon filets on the parchment and sprinkle with the salt and pepper and rub the spices into the fish.*
3. *Top the fish with the olive oil, asparagus, and lemon juice Sprinkle the parmesan on top along with the parsley.*
4. *Place the tray in the air fryer and bake for 20 minutes.*
5. *Remove from the air fryer and serve while hot!*

NUTRITION:

Calories 282, Total Fat 14g, Saturated Fat 5g, Total Carbs 11g, Net Carbs 6g, Protein 34g, Sugar 4g, Fiber 4g, Sodium 496mg, Potassium 325g

78. Parmesan Flounder and Asparagus

Preparation time: 20 minutes

Cooking time: 15 minutes Servings: 5

INGREDIENTS

- *1 ¾ pound flounder fillets*
- *¼ tsp salt*
- *¼ tsp ground black pepper*
- *3 Tbsp olive oil*
- *1 pound asparagus spears*
- *½ cup grated parmesan cheese*
- *1 Tbsp lemon juice*
- *1 Tbsp fresh chopped parsley*

DIRECTIONS

1. *Preheat your air fryer to 400 degrees F and line your air fryer tray with a long piece of parchment paper.*
2. *Place the flounder filets on the parchment and sprinkle with the salt and pepper and rub the spices into the fish.*
3. *Top the fish with the olive oil, asparagus, and lemon juice Sprinkle the parmesan on top along with the parsley.*
4. *Place the tray in the air fryer and bake*

for 15 minutes.

5. *Remove from the air fryer and serve while hot!*

NUTRITION:

Calories 269, Total Fat 13g, Saturated Fat 5g, Total Carbs 11g, Net Carbs 6g, Protein 32g, Sugar 4g, Fiber 4g, Sodium 496mg, Potassium 325g

79. Parmesan Salmon and Brussel Sprouts

Preparation time: 20 minutes

Cooking time: 20 minutes Servings: 5

INGREDIENTS

- *1 ¾ pound salmon fillets*
- *¼ tsp salt*
- *¼ tsp ground black pepper*
- *3 Tbsp olive oil*
- *1 pound sliced Brussel sprouts*
- *½ cup grated parmesan cheese*
- *1 Tbsp lemon juice*
- *1 Tbsp fresh chopped parsley*

DIRECTIONS

1. *Preheat your air fryer to 400 degrees F and line your air fryer tray with a long piece of parchment paper.*
2. *Place the salmon filets on the parchment and sprinkle with the salt and pepper and rub the spices into the fish.*
3. *Top the fish with the olive oil, Brussels sprouts, and lemon juice Sprinkle the parmesan on top along with the parsley.*
4. *Place the tray in the air fryer and bake for 20 minutes.*
5. *Remove from the air fryer and serve while hot!*

NUTRITION:

Calories 274, Total Fat 13g, Saturated Fat 5g, Total Carbs 11g, Net Carbs 6g, Protein 34g, Sugar 4g, Fiber 4g, Sodium 496mg, Potassium 325g

80. Parmesan Tuna and Brussel Sprouts

Preparation time: 20 minutes

Cooking time: 20 minutes Servings: 5

INGREDIENTS

- *1 ¾ pound tuna fillets*
- *¼ tsp salt*
- *¼ tsp ground black pepper*
- *3 Tbsp olive oil*
- *1 pound sliced Brussel sprouts*
- *½ cup grated parmesan cheese*
- *1 Tbsp lemon juice*
- *1 Tbsp fresh chopped parsley*

DIRECTIONS

1. *Preheat your air fryer to 400 degrees F and line your air fryer tray with a long piece of parchment paper.*
2. *Place the tuna filets on the parchment and sprinkle with the salt and pepper and rub the spices into the fish.*
3. *Top the fish with the olive oil, Brussels sprouts, and lemon juice Sprinkle the parmesan on top along with the parsley.*
4. *Place the tray in the air fryer and bake for 20 minutes.*
5. *Remove from the air fryer and serve while hot!*

NUTRITION:

Calories 285, Total Fat 13g, Saturated Fat 5g, Total Carbs 11g, Net Carbs 6g, Protein 34g, Sugar 4g, Fiber 4g, Sodium 496mg, Potassium 325g

81. Lemon Dill Wrapped Cod

Preparation time: 5 minutes

Cooking time: 15 minutes

Servings: 2

INGREDIENTS

- *1 pound cod fillets*
- *¼ tsp salt*
- *¼ tsp ground black pepper*
- *1 tsp lemon zest*
- *1 Tbsp chopped fresh dill*
- *2 oz prosciutto de parma, very thinly sliced*
- *2 Tbsp olive oil*
- *1 tsp minced garlic*
- *4 cups baby spinach*
- *2 tsp lemon juice*

DIRECTIONS

1. *Preheat your air fryer to 325 degrees F and line your air fryer tray with foil.*
2. *Dry the cod fillets by patting with a paper towel the sprinkle with salt and pepper.*
3. *Sprinkle the lemon zest and dill on the filets as well.*
4. *Wrap the filets in the prosciutto, enclosing them as fully as possible.*
5. *Place the wrapped filets on the prepared tray.*
6. *Toss the spinach with the olive oil, garlic and lemon juice and place on the tray as well, around the wrapped cod.*
7. *Place in the air fryer and bake for 12 minutes. The spinach should be nicely wilted and the fish 145 degrees F internally.*
8. *Serve hot!*

NUTRITION:

Calories 430, Total Fat 20g, Saturated Fat 3g, Total Carbs 11g, Net Carbs 9g, Protein 49g, Sugar 3g, Fiber 2g, Sodium 482mg, Potassium 582g

82. Mediterranean Salmon

Preparation time: 20 minutes

Cooking time: 20 minutes Servings: 5

INGREDIENTS

- *1 ¾ pound salmon fillets*
- *¼ tsp salt*
- *1 tsp smoked paprika*
- *1 tsp ground dried ginger*
- *¼ cup pitted olives*
- *¼ cup sundried tomatoes*
- *¼ cup capers*
- *1 Tbsp fresh chopped dill*
- *1/3 cup keto pesto sauce*

DIRECTIONS

1. *Preheat your air fryer to 400 degrees F and line your air fryer tray with a long piece of parchment paper.*
2. *Place the salmon filets on the parchment and sprinkle with the salt, paprika, and ginger and rub the spices into the fish.*
3. *Top the fish with the remaining ingredients and then wrap the parchment paper up around the fish filets, enclosing them completely.*
4. *Place the tray in the air fryer and bake for 20 minutes.*
5. *Remove from the air fryer, unwrap the parchment and serve while hot!*

NUTRITION:

Calories 243, Total Fat 10g, Saturated Fat 4g, Total Carbs 7g, Net Carbs 3g, Protein 33g, Sugar 1g, Fiber 4g, Sodium 489mg, Potassium 321g

83. Lemon Dill Parchment Salmon

Preparation time: 20 minutes

Cooking time: 20 minutes Servings: 5

INGREDIENTS

- *1 ¾ pound salmon fillets*
- *¼ tsp salt*
- *1 TBSP fresh chopped dill*
- *1 tsp lemon zest*
- *¼ cup pitted olives*
- *¼ cup sundried tomatoes*
- *¼ cup capers*
- *2 Tbsp olive oil*

DIRECTIONS

1. *Preheat your air fryer to 400 degrees F and line your air fryer tray with a long piece of parchment paper.*
2. *Place the salmon filets on the parchment and sprinkle with the salt, lemon zest, and dill and rub the spices into the fish.*
3. *Top the fish with the remaining ingredients and then wrap the parchment paper up around the fish filets, enclosing them completely.*
4. *Place the tray in the air fryer and bake for 20 minutes.*
5. *Remove from the air fryer, unwrap the parchment and serve while hot!*

NUTRITION:

Calories 214, Total Fat 10g, Saturated Fat 4g, Total Carbs 5g, Net Carbs 1g, Protein 33g, Sugar 1g, Fiber 4g, Sodium 489mg, Potassium 321g

84. Mediterranean Flounder

Preparation time: 20 minutes

Cooking time: 12 minutes Servings: 5

INGREDIENTS

- *1 ¾ pound salmon fillets*
- *¼ tsp salt*
- *1 tsp smoked paprika*
- *1 tsp ground dried ginger*
- *¼ cup pitted olives*
- *¼ cup sundried tomatoes*
- *¼ cup capers*
- *1 Tbsp fresh chopped dill*
- *1/3 cup keto pesto sauce*

DIRECTIONS

1. *Preheat your air fryer to 400 degrees F and line your air fryer tray with a long piece of parchment paper.*
2. *Place the flounder filets on the parchment and sprinkle with the salt, paprika, and ginger and rub the spices into the fish.*
3. *Top the fish with the remaining ingredients and then wrap the parchment paper up around the fish filets, enclosing them completely.*
4. *Place the tray in the air fryer and bake for 12 minutes.*
5. *Remove from the air fryer, unwrap the parchment and serve while hot!*

NUTRITION:

Calories 211, Total Fat 8g, Saturated Fat 3g, Total Carbs 6g, Net Carbs 3g, Protein 33g, Sugar 1g, Fiber 3g, Sodium 489mg, Potassium 321g

85. Tomato Parchment Cod

Preparation time: 20 minutes

Cooking time: 15 minutes Servings: 5

INGREDIENTS

- *1 ¾ pound cod fillets*
- *¼ tsp salt*
- *1 tsp smoked paprika*
- *1 tsp ground dried ginger*
- *¼ cup pitted olives*
- *¼ cup sundried tomatoes*
- *¼ cup capers*
- *1 Tbsp fresh chopped dill*
- *1/3 cup keto marinara*

DIRECTIONS

1. *Preheat your air fryer to 400 degrees F and line your air fryer tray with a long piece of parchment paper.*
2. *Place the cod filets on the parchment and sprinkle with the salt, paprika, and ginger and rub the spices into the fish.*
3. *Top the fish with the remaining ingredients and then wrap the parchment paper up around the fish filets, enclosing them completely.*
4. *Place the tray in the air fryer and bake for 15 minutes.*
5. *Remove from the air fryer, unwrap the parchment and serve while hot!*

NUTRITION:

Calories 373, Total Fat 7g, Saturated Fat 3g, Total Carbs 5g, Net Carbs 3g, Protein 33g, Sugar 1g, Fiber 2g, Sodium 489mg, Potassium 321g

86. Italian Style Flounder

Preparation time: 20 minutes

Cooking time: 15 minutes Servings: 5

INGREDIENTS

- *1 ¾ pound salmon fillets*
- *¼ tsp salt*
- *2 tsp Italian seasoning*
- *1 cup baby spinach*
- *¼ cup sundried tomatoes*
- *1 Tbsp fresh chopped dill*
- *1/3 cup keto pesto sauce*

DIRECTIONS

1. *Preheat your air fryer to 400 degrees F and line your air fryer tray with a long piece of parchment paper.*
2. *Place the flounder filets on the parchment and sprinkle with the salt and Italian seasoning and rub the spices into the fish.*
3. *Top the fish with the remaining ingredients and then wrap the parchment paper up around the fish filets, enclosing them completely.*
4. *Place the tray in the air fryer and bake for 20 minutes.*
5. *Remove from the air fryer, unwrap the parchment and serve while hot!*

NUTRITION:

Calories 226, Total Fat 8g, Saturated Fat 3g, Total Carbs 7g, Net Carbs 3g, Protein 30g, Sugar 2g, Fiber 4g, Sodium 487mg, Potassium 321g

87. Lemon Parchment Salmon

Preparation time: 20 minutes

Cooking time: 20 minutes

Servings: 5

INGREDIENTS

- *1 ¾ pound salmon fillets*
- *¼ tsp salt*
- *½ tsp ground black pepper*
- *2 cups baby spinach*
- *1 lemon, sliced thinly*

DIRECTIONS

1. *Preheat your air fryer to 400 degrees F and line your air fryer tray with a long piece of parchment paper.*
2. *Place the salmon filets on the parchment and sprinkle with the salt and pepper and rub the spices into the fish.*
3. *Top the fish with the remaining ingredients and then wrap the parchment paper up around the fish filets, enclosing them completely.*
4. *Place the tray in the air fryer and bake for 20 minutes.*
5. *Remove from the air fryer, unwrap the parchment and serve while hot!*

NUTRITION:

Calories 264, Total Fat 9g, Saturated Fat 4g, Total Carbs 8g, Net Carbs 3g, Protein 33g, Sugar 1g, Fiber 5g, Sodium 492mg, Potassium 324g

88. Prosciutto Wrapped Ahi Ahi

Preparation time: 5 minutes

Cooking time: 20 minutes Servings: 2

INGREDIENTS

- *1 pound cod Ahi Ahi*
- *¼ tsp salt*
- *¼ tsp ground black pepper*
- *2 oz prosciutto de parma, very thinly sliced*
- *2 Tbsp olive oil*
- *1 tsp minced garlic*
- *4 cups baby spinach*
- *2 tsp lemon juice*

DIRECTIONS

1. *Preheat your air fryer to 325 degrees F and line your air fryer tray with foil.*
2. *Dry the cod fillets by patting with a paper towel the sprinkle with salt and pepper.*
3. *Wrap the filets in the prosciutto, enclosing them as fully as possible.*
4. *Place the wrapped filets on the prepared tray.*
5. *Place the tray in the air fryer and bake for 10 minutes.*
6. *Toss the spinach with the olive oil, garlic and lemon juice and remove the tray from the air fryer and place the spinach mix on the tray as well, around the wrapped cod.*
7. *Place in the air fryer and bake for another 10 minutes. The spinach should be nicely wilted and the fish 145 degrees F internally.*
8. *Serve hot!*

NUTRITION:

Calories 420, Total Fat 20g, Saturated Fat 4g, Total Carbs 11g, Net Carbs 9g, Protein 49g, Sugar 3g, Fiber 2g, Sodium 480mg, Potassium 579g

89. Prosciutto Wrapped Tuna Bites

Preparation time: 5 minutes

Cooking time: 10 minutes Servings: 2

INGREDIENTS

- *1 pound tuna cut into 1" pieces*
- *¼ tsp salt*
- *¼ tsp ground black pepper*
- *2 oz prosciutto de parma, very thinly sliced*
- *2 Tbsp olive oil*
- *1 tsp minced garlic*
- *4 cups baby spinach*
- *2 tsp lemon juice*

DIRECTIONS

1. *Preheat your air fryer to 325 degrees F and line your air fryer tray with foil.*
2. *Dry the tuna bites by patting with a paper towel the sprinkle with salt and pepper.*
3. *Wrap the bites in the prosciutto, enclosing them as fully as possible.*
4. *Place the wrapped bites on the prepared tray.*
5. *Toss the spinach with the olive oil, garlic and lemon juice and place on the tray as well, around the wrapped tuna.*
6. *Place in the air fryer and bake for 12 minutes. The spinach should be nicely wilted and the fish 145 degrees F internally.*
7. *Serve hot!*

NUTRITION:

Calories 430, Total Fat 20g, Saturated Fat 3g, Total Carbs 11g, Net Carbs 9g, Protein 49g, Sugar 3g, Fiber 2g, Sodium 480mg, Potassium 580g

POULTRY

90. BBQ Chicken Patties

Preparation time: 30 minutes

Cooking time: 60 minutes Servings: 8

INGREDIENTS

- *10 oz shredded rotisserie chicken*
- *4 oz pork rinds, crushed*
- *½ cup mozzarella cheese, grated*
- *½ cup keto BBQ sauce*
- *2 eggs*
- *½ tsp smoked paprika*
- *3 Tbsp water*
- *2 Tbsp olive oil*

DIRECTIONS

1. *Preheat your air fryer to 375 degrees F and line your air fryer tray with foil or parchment.*
2. *Place all the ingredients except for the olive oil, in a large bowl and blend together well using your hands.*
3. *Cover the bowl and refrigerate for an hour to let the flavors soak together.*
4. *Remove the bowl from the fridge and use your hands to form the tuna cakes, making each patty about one inch thick.*
5. *Place the cakes on the prepared sheet tray and drizzle with the olive oil.*
6. *Cook the cakes in the air fryer for about 7 minutes or until golden browned.*
7. *Remove from the air fryer and serve while hot.*

NUTRITION: *Calories 367, Total Fat 30g, Saturated Fat 8g, Total Carbs 6g, Net Carbs 4g, Protein 30g, Sugar 2g, Fiber 2g, Sodium 378mg, Potassium 213g*

91. Lemon Pepper Chicken Patties

Preparation time: 30 minutes Cooking time: 60 minutes Servings: 8

INGREDIENTS

- *10 shredded, cooked chicken*
- *4 oz pork rinds, crushed*
- *1 cup mozzarella cheese, grated*
- *1 Tbsp keto mayonnaise*
- *2 eggs*
- *½ tsp ground black pepper*
- *1 Tbsp lemon zest*
- *3 Tbsp water*
- *2 Tbsp olive oil*

DIRECTIONS

1. *Preheat your air fryer to 375 degrees F and line your air fryer tray with foil or parchment.*
2. *Place all the ingredients except for the olive oil, in a large bowl and blend together well using your hands.*
3. *Cover the bowl and refrigerate for an hour to let the flavors soak together.*
4. *Remove the bowl from the fridge and use your hands to form the tuna cakes, making each patty about one inch thick.*
5. *Place the cakes on the prepared sheet tray and drizzle with the olive oil.*
6. *Cook the cakes in the air fryer for about 7 minutes or until golden browned.*
7. *Remove from the air fryer and serve while hot.*

NUTRITION: *Calories 341, Total Fat 29g, Saturated Fat 9g, Total Carbs 1g, Net Carbs 1g, Protein 30g, Sugar 1g, Fiber 0g, Sodium 301mg, Potassium 194g*

92. Garlic Chicken Patties

Preparation time: 30 minutes

Cooking time: 60 minutes Servings: 8

INGREDIENTS

- *10 shredded, cooked chicken*
- *4 oz pork rinds, crushed*
- *1 cup mozzarella cheese, grated*
- *1 Tbsp keto mayonnaise*
- *2 eggs*
- *1 tsp garlic powder*
- *1 Tbsp minced garlic*
- *3 Tbsp water*
- *2 Tbsp olive oil*

DIRECTIONS

1. *Preheat your air fryer to 375 degrees F and line your air fryer tray with foil or*

   parchment.
2. *Place all the ingredients except for the olive oil, in a large bowl and blend together well using your hands.*
3. *Cover the bowl and refrigerate for an hour to let the flavors soak together.*
4. *Remove the bowl from the fridge and use your hands to form the tuna cakes, making each patty about one inch thick.*
5. *Place the cakes on the prepared sheet tray and drizzle with the olive oil.*
6. *Cook the cakes in the air fryer for about 7 minutes or until golden browned.*
7. *Remove from the air fryer and serve while hot.*

NUTRITION: *Calories 352, Total Fat 28g, Saturated Fat 8g, Total Carbs 2g, Net Carbs 2g, Protein 30g, Sugar 2g, Fiber 0g, Sodium 316mg, Potassium 202g*

93. Prosciutto Wrapped Chicken

Preparation time: 5 minutes

Cooking time: 15 minutes Servings: 2

INGREDIENTS

- *1 pound chicken breast*
- *¼ tsp salt*
- *¼ tsp ground black pepper*
- *2 oz prosciutto de parma, very thinly sliced*
- *2 Tbsp olive oil*
- *1 tsp minced garlic*
- *4 cups baby spinach*
- *2 tsp lemon juice*

DIRECTIONS

1. *Preheat your air fryer to 325 degrees F and line your air fryer tray with foil.*
2. *Dry the chicken by patting with a paper towel then cut into strips and sprinkle with salt and pepper.*
3. *Wrap the chicken breast in the prosciutto, enclosing them as fully as possible.*
4. *Place the wrapped chicken breast on the prepared tray.*
5. *Toss the spinach with the olive oil, garlic and lemon juice and place on the tray as well, around the wrapped chicken.*
6. *Place in the air fryer and bake for 12 minutes. The spinach should be nicely wilted and the chicken 145 degrees F internally.*
7. *Serve hot!*

NUTRITION: *Calories 437, Total Fat 17g, Saturated Fat 3g, Total Carbs 11g, Net Carbs 9g, Protein 41g, Sugar 3g, Fiber 2g, Sodium 482mg, Potassium 582g*

94. Pepper and Prosciutto Chicken

Preparation time: 5 minutes

Cooking time: 15 minutes

Servings: 2

INGREDIENTS

- *1 pound chicken breast*
- *¼ tsp salt*
- *½ tsp ground black pepper*
- *2 oz prosciutto de parma, very thinly sliced*
- *2 Tbsp olive oil*
- *1 tsp minced garlic*
- *4 cups baby spinach*
- *2 tsp lemon juice*

DIRECTIONS

1. *Preheat your air fryer to 325 degrees F and line your air fryer tray with foil.*
2. *Dry the chicken by patting with a paper towel then cut into strips and sprinkle with salt and pepper.*
3. *Wrap the chicken breast in the prosciutto, enclosing them as fully as possible.*
4. *Place the wrapped chicken breast on the prepared tray.*
5. *Toss the spinach with the olive oil, garlic and lemon juice and place on the tray as well, around the wrapped chicken.*
6. *Place in the air fryer and bake for 12 minutes. The spinach should be nicely wilted and the fish 145 degrees F internally.*
7. *Serve hot!*

NUTRITION: *Calories 437, Total Fat 17g, Saturated Fat 3g, Total Carbs 11g, Net Carbs 9g, Protein 41g, Sugar 3g, Fiber 2g, Sodium 482mg, Potassium 582g*

95. Roasted Chicken Thighs

Preparation time: 20 minutes

Cooking time: 30 minutes

Servings: 6

INGREDIENTS

- *2 pounds chicken thighs, bone in, skin on*
- *½ tsp salt*
- *½ tsp ground black pepper*
- *3 carrots, chopped*
- *2 celery stalks, chopped*
- *1 Tbsp minced garlic*
- *3 Tbsp butter, melted*
- *½ cup white onion, chopped*
- *1 tsp dried thyme*
- *½ tsp dried rosemary*

DIRECTIONS

1. *Preheat your air fryer to 425 degrees F and prepare your air fryer tray with a piece of foil.*
2. *Rub the chicken thighs with the salt and pepper, wrap and let sit overnight to season.*
3. *Place the onion, carrot, celery and garlic on the prepared foil lined tray.*
4. *Place the chicken thighs on top of the veggies.*
5. *Brush the chicken with the melted butter and sprinkle with the thyme and rosemary.*
6. *Bake in the air fryer for 20 minutes or until the chicken thighs are browned and the veggies are beginning to brown as well.*
7. *Serve hot.*

NUTRITION: *Calories 243, Total Fat 12g, Saturated Fat 5g, Total Carbs 4g, Net Carbs 3g, Protein 30g, Sugar 2g, Fiber 1g, Sodium 350mg, Potassium 104g*

96. Dijon Roasted Chicken Thighs

Preparation time: 20 minutes

Cooking time: 30 minutes Servings: 6

INGREDIENTS

- *2 pounds chicken thighs, bone in, skin on*
- *½ tsp salt*
- *½ tsp ground black pepper*
- *¼ cup Dijon mustard*
- *3 carrots, chopped*
- *2 celery stalks, chopped*
- *1 Tbsp minced garlic*
- *3 Tbsp butter, melted*
- *½ cup white onion, chopped*
- *1 tsp dried thyme*
- *½ tsp dried rosemary*

DIRECTIONS

1. *Preheat your air fryer to 425 degrees F and prepare your air fryer tray with a piece of foil.*
2. *Rub the chicken thighs with the salt, pepper and Dijon mustard, wrap and let sit overnight to season.*
3. *Place the onion, carrot, celery and garlic on the prepared foil lined tray.*
4. *Place the chicken thighs on top of the veggies.*
5. *Brush the chicken with the melted butter and sprinkle with the thyme and rosemary.*
6. *Bake in the air fryer for 20 minutes or until the chicken thighs are browned and the veggies are beginning to brown as well.*
7. *Serve hot.*

NUTRITION: *Calories 256, Total Fat 13g, Saturated Fat 5g, Total Carbs 5g, Net Carbs 4g, Protein 30g, Sugar 3g, Fiber 1g, Sodium 350mg, Potassium 104g*

97. Cajun Roasted Chicken Thighs

Preparation time: 20 minutes

Cooking time: 30 minutes Servings: 6

INGREDIENTS

- *2 pounds chicken thighs, bone in, skin on*
- *½ tsp salt*
- *1 tsp Cajun seasoning*
- *3 carrots, chopped*
- *2 celery stalks, chopped*
- *1 Tbsp minced garlic*
- *3 Tbsp butter, melted*
- *½ cup white onion, chopped*
- *1 tsp dried thyme*
- *½ tsp dried rosemary*

DIRECTIONS

1. *Preheat your air fryer to 425 degrees F and prepare your air fryer tray with a piece of foil.*
2. *Rub the chicken thighs with the salt and Cajun seasoning, wrap and let sit overnight to season.*
3. *Place the onion, carrot, celery and garlic on the prepared foil lined tray.*
4. *Place the chicken thighs on top of the veggies.*
5. *Brush the chicken with the melted butter and sprinkle with the thyme and rosemary.*
6. *Bake in the air fryer for 20 minutes or until the chicken thighs are browned and the veggies are beginning to brown as well.*
7. *Serve hot.*

NUTRITION: *Calories 245, Total Fat 12g, Saturated Fat 5g, Total Carbs 4g, Net Carbs 3g, Protein 30g, Sugar 2g, Fiber 1g, Sodium 353mg, Potassium 104g*

98. Lemon Roasted Chicken Thighs

Preparation time: 20 minutes

Cooking time: 30 minutes Servings: 6

INGREDIENTS

- *2 pounds chicken thighs, bone in, skin on*
- *½ tsp salt*
- *½ tsp ground black pepper*
- *3 carrots, chopped*
- *2 celery stalks, chopped*
- *1 Tbsp minced garlic*
- *3 Tbsp butter, melted*
- *½ cup white onion, chopped*
- *1 tsp dried thyme*
- *½ tsp dried rosemary*
- *1 lemon, sliced thinly*

DIRECTIONS

1. *Preheat your air fryer to 425 degrees F and prepare your air fryer tray with a piece of foil.*
2. *Rub the chicken thighs with the salt and pepper, wrap and let sit overnight to season.*
3. *Place the onion, carrot, celery, lemon slices and garlic on the prepared foil lined tray.*
4. *Place the chicken thighs on top of the veggies.*
5. *Brush the chicken with the melted butter and sprinkle with the thyme and rosemary.*
6. *Bake in the air fryer for 20 minutes or until the chicken thighs are browned and the veggies are beginning to brown as well.*
7. *Serve hot.*

NUTRITION:

Calories 252, Total Fat 12g, Saturated Fat 5g, Total Carbs 6g, Net Carbs 4g, Protein 30g, Sugar 2g, Fiber 2g, Sodium 350mg, Potassium 119g

99. Roasted Chicken Thighs and Brussels

Cooking time: 30 minutes Preparation time: 20 minutes

Servings: 6

INGREDIENTS

- *2pounds chicken thighs, bone in, skin on*
- *½ tsp salt*
- *½ tsp ground blackpepper*
- *3 carrots, chopped*
- *2 celery stalks, chopped*
- *4 cups sliced Brussels sprouts*
- *1 Tbsp minced garlic*
- *3 Tbsp butter, melted*
- *½ cup white onion, chopped*
- *1 tsp dried thyme*
- *½ tsp dried rosemary*

DIRECTIONS

1. *Preheat your air fryer to 425 degrees F and prepare your air fryer tray with a piece of foil.*
2. *Rub the chicken thighs with the salt and pepper, wrap and let sit overnight to season.*
3. *Place the onion, carrot, celery, Brussels sprouts and garlic on the prepared foil lined tray.*
4. *Place the chicken thighs on top of the veggies.*
5. *Brush the chicken with the melted butter and sprinkle with the thyme and rosemary.*
6. *Bake in the air fryer for 20 minutes or until the chicken thighs are browned and the veggies are beginning to brown as well.*
7. *Serve hot.*

NUTRITION: *Calories 277, Total Fat 12g, Saturated Fat 5g, Total Carbs 10g, Net Carbs 4g, Protein 30g, Sugar 3g, Fiber 6g, Sodium 386mg, Potassium 104g*

100. Maple Roasted Chicken Thighs

Preparation time: 20 minutes

Cooking time: 30 minutes Servings: 6

INGREDIENTS

- *2 pounds chicken thighs, bone in, skin on*
- *½ tsp salt*
- *½ tsp ground black pepper*
- *1 tsp maple extract*
- *3 carrots, chopped*
- *2 celery stalks, chopped*
- *1 Tbsp minced garlic*
- *3 Tbsp butter, melted*
- *½ cup white onion, chopped*
- *1 tsp dried thyme*
- *½ tsp dried rosemary*

DIRECTIONS

1. *Preheat your air fryer to 425 degrees F and prepare your air fryer tray with a piece of foil.*
2. *Rub the chicken thighs with the salt, pepper, and maple extract, wrap and let sit overnight to season.*
3. *Place the onion, carrot, celery and garlic on the prepared foil lined tray.*
4. *Place the chicken thighs on top of the veggies.*
5. *Brush the chicken with the melted butter and sprinkle with the thyme and rosemary.*
6. *Bake in the air fryer for 20 minutes or until the chicken thighs are browned and the veggies are beginning to brown as well.*
7. *Serve hot.*

NUTRITION: *Calories 243, Total Fat 12g, Saturated Fat 5g, Total Carbs 4g, Net Carbs 3g, Protein 30g, Sugar 2g, Fiber 1g, Sodium 350mg, Potassium 104g*

101. Prosciutto and Lemon Chicken

Servings: 2
Preparation time: 5 minutes Cooking time: 15 minutes

INGREDIENTS

- *1 pound chicken breast*
- *¼ tsp salt*
- *¼ tsp ground black pepper*
- *2 oz prosciutto de parma, very thinly sliced*
- *½ lemon sliced thinly*
- *2 Tbsp olive oil*
- *1 tsp minced garlic*
- *4 cups baby spinach*
- *2 tsp lemon juice*

DIRECTIONS

1. *Preheat your air fryer to 325 degrees F and line your air fryer tray with foil.*
2. *Dry the chicken by patting with a paper towel then cut into strips and sprinkle with salt and pepper.*
3. *Wrap the chicken breast in the prosciutto, enclosing them as fully as possible.*
4. *Place the wrapped chicken breast on the prepared tray and place the lemon slices on top of each wrap.*
5. *Toss the spinach with the olive oil, garlic and lemon juice and place on the tray as well, around the wrapped chicken.*
6. *Place in the air fryer and bake for 12 minutes. The spinach should be nicely wilted and the fish 145 degrees F internally.*
7. *Serve hot!*

NUTRITION: *Calories 449, Total Fat 17g, Saturated Fat 3g, Total Carbs 14g, Net Carbs 12g, Protein 41g, Sugar 4g, Fiber 2g, Sodium 482mg, Potassium 582g*

102. Blackened Chicken Patties

Preparation time: 30 minutes Cooking time: 60 minutes
Servings: 8

INGREDIENTS

- *10 shredded, cooked chicken*
- *4 oz pork rinds, crushed*
- *1 cup mozzarella cheese, grated*
- *1 Tbsp keto mayonnaise*
- *2 eggs*
- *½ tsp smoked paprika*
- *1 Tbsp activated charcoal*
- *3 Tbsp water*
- *2 Tbsp olive oil*

DIRECTIONS

1. *Preheat your air fryer to 375 degrees F and line your air fryer tray with foil or parchment.*
2. *Place all the ingredients except for the olive oil, in a large bowl and blend together well using your hands.*
3. *Cover the bowl and refrigerate for an hour to let the flavors soak together.*
4. *Remove the bowl from the fridge and use your hands to form the tuna cakes, making each patty about one inch thick.*
5. *Place the cakes on the prepared sheet tray and drizzle with the olive oil.*
6. *Cook the cakes in the air fryer for about 7 minutes or until golden browned.*
7. *Remove from the air fryer and serve while hot.*

NUTRITION: *Calories 345, Total Fat 28g, Saturated Fat 8g, Total Carbs 1g, Net Carbs 1g, Protein 30g, Sugar 1g, Fiber 0g, Sodium 301mg, Potassium 194g*

103. Garlic Chicken Bacon Bake

Preparation time: 10 minutes

Cooking time: 10 minutes Servings: 4

INGREDIENTS

- *¼ cup butter*
- *2 Tbsp minced garlic*
- *1 pound cooked, shredded chicken*
- *¼ tsp ground black pepper*
- *½ cup cooked, chopped bacon*
- *1/3 cup heavy cream*
- *¼ cup parmesan cheese*

DIRECTIONS

1. *Preheat your air fryer to 400 degrees F and grease an 8x8 inch baking pan.*
2. *Add the butter and chicken to the pan and place in the air fryer for 3 minutes. Remove the pan from the air fryer.*
3. *Add the remaining ingredients to the pan and return to the air fryer to cook for another 5 minutes. The mix should be bubbling.*
4. *Serve with zucchini noodles or enjoy plain.*

NUTRITION: *Calories 302, Total Fat 21g,*

Saturated Fat 13g, Total Carbs 3g, Net Carbs 3g, Protein 31g, Sugar 0g, Fiber 0g, Sodium 924mg, Potassium 24g

104. Garlic Chicken Bake

Preparation time: 10 minutes

Cooking time: 10 minutes Servings: 4

INGREDIENTS

- *¼ cup butter*
- *2 Tbsp minced garlic*
- *1 pound cooked, shredded chicken*
- *¼ tsp ground black pepper*
- *1/3 cup heavy cream*
- *¼ cup parmesan cheese*

DIRECTIONS

1. *Preheat your air fryer to 400 degrees F and grease an 8x8 inch baking pan.*
2. *Add the butter and chicken to the pan and place in the air fryer for 3 minutes. Remove the pan from the air fryer.*
3. *Add the remaining ingredients to the pan and return to the air fryer to cook for another 5 minutes. The mix should be bubbling.*
4. *Serve with zucchini noodles or enjoy plain.*

NUTRITION: *Calories 273, Total Fat 16g, Saturated Fat 9g, Total Carbs 3g, Net Carbs 3g, Protein 25g, Sugar 0g, Fiber 0g, Sodium 432mg, Potassium 24g*

105. Spicy Chicken Bacon Bake

Preparation time: 10 minutes

Cooking time: 10 minutes

Servings: 4

INGREDIENTS

- *¼ cup butter*
- *2 Tbsp minced garlic*
- *1 pound cooked, shredded chicken*
- *1 tsp cayenne seasoning*
- *½ cup cooked, chopped bacon*
- *1/3 cup heavy cream*
- *¼ cup parmesan cheese*

DIRECTIONS

1. *Preheat your air fryer to 400 degrees F and grease an 8x8 inch baking pan.*
2. *Add the butter and chicken to the pan and place in the air fryer for 3 minutes. Remove the pan from the air fryer.*
3. *Add the remaining ingredients to the pan and return to the air fryer to cook for another 5 minutes. The mix should be bubbling.*
4. *Serve with zucchini noodles or enjoy plain.*

NUTRITION: *Calories 301, Total Fat 21g, Saturated Fat 13g, Total Carbs 3g, Net Carbs 3g, Protein 31g, Sugar 0g, Fiber 0g, Sodium 929mg, Potassium 24g*

106. Chicken Zucchini Boats

Preparation time: 20 minutes

Cooking time: 20 minutes Servings: 6

INGREDIENTS

- *3 zucchini, sliced in half, seeds scooped out*
- *1 tsp salt*
- *½ tsp ground black pepper*
- *1 tsp olive oil*
- *2 tsp smoked paprika*
- *1 cup chopped mushrooms*
- *1 cup cooked, shredded chicken (rotisserie chicken works well!)*
- *1 cup shredded cheddar cheese*
- *3 Tbsp sour cream*
- *2 Tbsp chopped chives*

DIRECTIONS

1. *Preheat your air fryer to 375 degrees F and line the air fryer tray or baking pan with foil.*
2. *Place the zucchini skins on the prepared tray and sprinkle with the salt. Let sit for*
3. *30 minutes then pat the skins dry to remove the water which the salt has extracted.*
4. *Spread the mushrooms inside the zucchini boats, dividing the filling evenly.*
5. *Sprinkle the zucchini with the black pepper, paprika and olive oil.*
6. *Bake for 10 minutes to soften.*
7. *Remove from the air fryer and top with the shredded chicken and cheese. Return to the air fryer for another 10 minutes or until the cheese is bubbly.*
8. *Remove from the air fryer and top with*

the sour cream and chives. Serve hot NUTRITION: *Calories 187, Total Fat 18g, Saturated Fat 9g, Total Carbs 7g, Net Carbs 3g, Protein 12g, Sugar 3g, Fiber 4g, Sodium 515mg, Potassium 219g*

MEAT

107. Brussels, Tomatoes and Pork Chops

Preparation time: 20 minutes

Cooking time: 30 minutes Servings: 4

INGREDIENTS

- *3 Tbsp olive oil*
- *3 Tbsp lemon juice*
- *3 Tbsp minced garlic*
- *1 tsp oregano, dried*
- *1 pound pork chops*
- *½ tsp sea salt*
- *¼ tsp ground black pepper*
- *1 pound Brussel sprouts sliced in half*
- *¼ cup chopped sundried tomatoes*
- *1 lemon, sliced thinly*

DIRECTIONS

1. *Preheat your air fryer to 400 degrees F and prepare your air fryer tray with a piece of foil.*
2. *In a large bowl, whisk together 2 Tbsp of the olive oil, lemon juice, dried oregano and garlic.*
3. *Add the pork chops to the bowl and toss to coat. Cover the bowl and place in the fridge for two hours.*
4. *Add the remaining tablespoon of olive oil to a saute pan and heat over high. Sear the marinated pork chops on each side for 3 minutes, just to brown.*
5. *Move the browned pork chops to the prepared, foil lined tray and pour the remaining marinade from the bowl over the chops.*
6. *Add the Brussels, sundried tomatoes and lemon slices, layering them over and around the pork chops.*
7. *Place the tray in the preheated air fryer for 20 minutes. Serve hot.*

NUTRITION: *Calories 253, Total Fat 10g, Saturated Fat 2g, Total Carbs 11g, Net Carbs 6g, Protein 27g, Sugar 4g, Fiber 5g, Sodium 388mg, Potassium 232g*

108. Veggies Roasted Pork Chops

Preparation time: 20 minutes

Cooking time: 30

minutes Servings: 6

INGREDIENTS

- *2 pounds Pork Chops, bone-in*
- *½ tsp salt*
- *½ tsp ground black pepper*
- *3 carrots, chopped*
- *2 celery stalks, chopped*
- *1 Tbsp minced garlic*
- *3 Tbsp butter, melted*
- *½ cup white onion, chopped*
- *1 tsp dried thyme*
- *½ tsp dried rosemary*

DIRECTIONS

1. *Preheat your air fryer to 425 degrees F and prepare your air fryer tray with a piece of foil.*
2. *Rub the pork chops with the salt and pepper, wrap and let sit overnight to season.*
3. *Place the onion, carrot, celery and garlic on the prepared foil lined tray.*
4. *Place the pork chops on top of the veggies.*
5. *Brush the pork chops with the melted butter and sprinkle with the thyme and rosemary.*
6. *Bake in the air fryer for 30 minutes or until the chicken thighs are browned and the veggies are beginning to brown as well.*
7. *Serve hot.*

NUTRITION: *Calories 243, Total Fat 12g, Saturated Fat 6g, Total Carbs 6g, Net Carbs 5g, Protein 31g, Sugar 3g, Fiber 1g, Sodium 496mg, Potassium 104g*

109. Dijon Roasted Pork Chops

Preparation time: 20 minutes

Cooking time: 30 minutes

Servings: 6

INGREDIENTS

- *2 pounds Pork Chops, bone-in*
- *½ tsp salt*
- *½ tsp ground black pepper*
- *¼ cup Dijon mustard*
- *3 carrots, chopped*
- *2 celery stalks, chopped*
- *1 Tbsp minced garlic*
- *3 Tbsp butter, melted*
- *½ cup white onion, chopped*
- *1 tsp dried thyme*
- *½ tsp dried rosemary*

DIRECTIONS

1. *Preheat your air fryer to 425 degrees F and prepare your air fryer tray with a piece of foil.*
2. *Rub the pork chops with the salt, pepper, and Dijon and wrap and let sit overnight to season.*
3. *Place the onion, carrot, celery and garlic on the prepared foil lined tray.*
4. *Place the pork chops on top of the veggies.*
5. *Brush the pork chops with the melted butter and sprinkle with the thyme and rosemary.*
6. *Bake in the air fryer for 30 minutes or until the chicken thighs are browned and the veggies are beginning to brown as well.*
7. *Serve hot.*

NUTRITION: *Calories 254, Total Fat 13g, Saturated Fat 6g, Total Carbs 8g, Net Carbs 7g, Protein 31g, Sugar 4g, Fiber 1g, Sodium 504mg, Potassium 110g*

110. Maple Roasted Pork Chops and Veggies

Preparation time: 20 minutes

Cooking time: 30 minutes Servings: 6

INGREDIENTS

- *2 pounds Pork Chops, bone-in*
- *½ tsp salt*
- *½ tsp ground black pepper*
- *1 tsp maple extract*
- *3 carrots, chopped*
- *2 celery stalks, chopped*
- *1 Tbsp minced garlic*
- *3 Tbsp butter, melted*
- *½ cup white onion, chopped*
- *1 tsp dried thyme*
- *½ tsp dried rosemary*

DIRECTIONS

1. *Preheat your air fryer to 425 degrees F and prepare your air fryer tray with a piece of foil.*
2. *Rub the pork chops with the salt, pepper, and maple extract and wrap and let sit overnight to season.*
3. *Place the onion, carrot, celery and garlic on the prepared foil lined tray.*
4. *Place the pork chops on top of the veggies.*
5. *Brush the pork chops with the melted butter and sprinkle with the thyme and rosemary.*
6. *Bake in the air fryer for 30 minutes or until the chicken thighs are browned and the veggies are beginning to brown as well.*
7. *Serve hot.*

NUTRITION: *Calories 243, Total Fat 12g, Saturated Fat 6g, Total Carbs 6g, Net Carbs 5g, Protein 31g, Sugar 3g, Fiber 1g, Sodium 496mg, Potassium 104g*

111. Brussels and Roasted Pork Chops

Preparation time: 20 minutes

Cooking time: 30 minutes Servings: 6

INGREDIENTS

- *2 pounds Pork Chops, bone-in*
- *½ tsp salt*
- *½ tsp ground black pepper*
- *3 carrots, chopped*
- *2 celery stalks, chopped*
- *½ pound Brussels Sprouts, sliced in half*
- *1 Tbsp minced garlic*
- *3 Tbsp butter, melted*
- *½ cup white onion, chopped*
- *1 tsp dried thyme*
- *½ tsp dried rosemary*

DIRECTIONS

1. *Preheat your air fryer to 425 degrees F and prepare your air fryer tray with a piece of foil.*
2. *Rub the pork chops with the salt and pepper, wrap and let sit overnight to season.*
3. *Place the onion, carrot, celery, Brussels and garlic on the prepared foil lined tray.*
4. *Place the pork chops on top of the veggies.*
5. *Brush the pork chops with the melted butter and sprinkle with the thyme and rosemary.*
6. *Bake in the air fryer for 30 minutes or until the chicken thighs are browned and the veggies are beginning to brown as well.*
7. *Serve hot.*

NUTRITION: *Calories 289, Total Fat 12g, Saturated Fat 6g, Total Carbs 11g, Net Carbs 9g, Protein 31g, Sugar 5g, Fiber 2g, Sodium 496mg, Potassium 104g*

112. Sweet Veggies Roasted Pork Chops

Preparation time: 20 minutes

Cooking time: 30 minutes Servings: 6

INGREDIENTS

- *2 pounds Pork Chops, bone-in*
- *½ tsp salt*
- *½ tsp ground black pepper*
- *3 carrots, chopped*
- *2 celery stalks, chopped*
- *1 Tbsp minced garlic*
- *3 Tbsp butter, melted*
- *2 Tbsp erythritol sweetener*
- *½ cup white onion, chopped*
- *1 tsp dried thyme*
- *½ tsp dried rosemary*

DIRECTIONS

1. *Preheat your air fryer to 425 degrees F and prepare your air fryer tray with a piece of foil.*
2. *Rub the pork chops with the salt and pepper, wrap and let sit overnight to season.*
3. *Place the onion, carrot, celery and garlic on the prepared foil lined tray. Sprinkle the erythritol over the veggies.*
4. *Place the pork chops on top of the veggies.*
5. *Brush the pork chops with the melted butter and sprinkle with the thyme and rosemary.*
6. *Bake in the air fryer for 30 minutes or*

   until the chicken thighs are browned and the veggies are beginning to brown as well.
7. *Serve hot.*

NUTRITION: *Calories 243, Total Fat 12g, Saturated Fat 6g, Total Carbs 6g, Net Carbs 5g, Protein 31g, Sugar 3g, Fiber 1g, Sodium 496mg, Potassium 104g*

113. Spinach and Bacon Casserole

Preparation time: 10 minutes

Cooking time: 30 minutes Servings: 12

INGREDIENTS

- *16 eggs*
- *¼ cup whole milk*
- *1 cup cooked, sliced bacon*
- *10 oz frozen, chopped spinach, thawed, drained*
- *1 cup cheddar cheese, grated*
- *½ cup grated parmesan cheese*
- *½ cup whole milk ricotta*
- *¼ cup chopped white onion*
- *1 tsp minced garlic*
- *1 tsp sea salt*
- *½ tsp dried thyme*
- *½ tsp ground black pepper*

DIRECTIONS

1. *Preheat your air fryer to 350 degrees F and prepare a large baking dish with baking grease (make sure the pan will fit in your air fryer.*
2. *Whisk the eggs and milk in a large bowl.*
3. *Add the bacon and spinach to the egg mix.*
4. *Add all the remaining ingredients, except the ricotta, and stir well.*
5. *Pour the egg and veggie mix into the prepared tray.*
6. *Dollop the ricotta around the pan, dispersing it evenly.*
7. *Bake in the air fryer for 30 minutes or until the eggs are completely set.*

NUTRITION: *Calories 319, Total Fat 22g, Saturated Fat 8g, Total Carbs 4g, Net Carbs 3g, Protein 20g, Sugar 3g, Fiber 1g, Sodium 689mg, Potassium 222g*

114. Asparagus and Bacon Casserole

Preparation time: 10 minutes

Cooking time: 30 minutes Servings: 12

INGREDIENTS

- *16 eggs*
- *¼ cup whole milk*
- *1 cup cooked, sliced bacon*
- *10 oz frozen, chopped spinach, thawed, drained*
- *1 cup cheddar cheese, grated*
- *½ cup grated parmesan cheese*
- *½ cup whole milk ricotta*
- *¼ cup chopped white onion*
- *1 tsp minced garlic*
- *1 tsp sea salt*
- *½ tsp dried thyme*
- *½ tsp ground black pepper*

DIRECTIONS

1. *Preheat your air fryer to 350 degrees F and prepare a large baking dish with baking grease (make sure the pan will fit in your air fryer.*
2. *Whisk the eggs and milk in a large bowl.*
3. *Add the bacon and asparagus to the egg mix.*
4. *Add all the remaining ingredients, except the ricotta, and stir well.*
5. *Pour the egg and veggie mix into the prepared tray.*
6. *Dollop the ricotta around the pan, dispersing it evenly.*
7. *Bake in the air fryer for 30 minutes or until the eggs are completely set.*

115. Spinach and Maple Bacon Casserole

Preparation time: 10 minutes

Cooking time: 30 minutes Servings: 12

INGREDIENTS

- *16 eggs*
- *¼ cup whole milk*
- *1 cup cooked, sliced bacon*
- *1 pound chopped asparagus*
- *1 cup cheddar cheese, grated*
- *½ cup grated parmesan cheese*
- *½ cup whole milk ricotta*
- *¼ cup chopped white onion*
- *1 tsp minced garlic*
- *1 tsp sea salt*
- *½ tsp dried thyme*
- *½ tsp ground black pepper DIRECTIONS*

1. *Preheat your air fryer to 350 degrees F and prepare a large baking dish with baking grease (make sure the pan will fit in your air fryer.*
2. *Whisk the eggs and milk in a large bowl.*
3. *Add the bacon and asparagus to the egg mix.*

NUTRITION: *Calories 322, Total Fat 22g, Saturated Fat 8g, Total Carbs 5g, Net Carbs 3g, Protein 20g, Sugar 3g, Fiber 2g, Sodium 689mg, Potassium 222g*

116. Spinach and Maple Bacon Casserole

Preparation time: 10 minutes

Cooking time: 30 minutes Servings: 12

INGREDIENTS

- *16 eggs*
- *¼ cup whole milk*
- *1 cup cooked, sliced maple seasoned bacon*
- *10 oz frozen, chopped spinach, thawed, drained*
- *1 cup cheddar cheese, grated*
- *½ cup grated parmesan cheese*
- *½ cup whole milk ricotta*
- *¼ cup chopped white onion*
- *1 tsp minced garlic*
- *1 tsp sea salt*
- *½ tsp dried thyme*
- *½ tsp ground black pepper*

DIRECTIONS

1. *Preheat your air fryer to 350 degrees F and prepare a large baking dish with baking grease (make sure the pan will fit in your air fryer.*
2. *Whisk the eggs and milk in a large bowl.*
3. *Add the bacon and spinach to the egg mix.*
4. *Add all the remaining ingredients, except the ricotta, and stir well.*
5. *Pour the egg and veggie mix into the prepared tray.*
6. *Dollop the ricotta around the pan,*

dispersing it evenly.

7. *Bake in the air fryer for 30 minutes or until the eggs are completely set.*

NUTRITION: *Calories 368, Total Fat 22g, Saturated Fat 8g, Total Carbs 9g, Net Carbs 8g, Protein 20g, Sugar 5g, Fiber 1g, Sodium 689mg, Potassium 222g*

117. Bacon and Cheese Casserole

Preparation time: 10 minutes

Cooking time: 30 minutes Servings: 12

INGREDIENTS

- *16 eggs*
- *¼ cup whole milk*
- *1 cup cooked, sliced maple seasoned bacon*
- *10 oz frozen, chopped spinach, thawed, drained*
- *1 cup cheddar cheese, grated*
- *½ cup grated parmesan cheese*
- *½ cup whole milk ricotta*
- *¼ cup chopped white onion*
- *1 tsp minced garlic*
- *1 tsp sea salt*
- *½ tsp dried thyme*
- *½ tsp ground black pepper*

DIRECTIONS

1. *Preheat your air fryer to 350 degrees F and prepare a large baking dish with baking grease (make sure the pan will fit in your air fryer.*
2. *Whisk the eggs and milk in a large bowl.*
3. *Add the bacon to the egg mix.*
4. *Add all the remaining ingredients, except the ricotta, and stir well.*
5. *Pour the egg and veggie mix into the prepared tray.*
6. *Dollop the ricotta around the pan, dispersing it evenly.*
7. *Bake in the air fryer for 30 minutes or until the eggs are completely set.*

NUTRITION: *Calories 301, Total Fat 22g, Saturated Fat 8g, Total Carbs 4g, Net Carbs 3g, Protein 20g, Sugar 3g, Fiber 1g, Sodium 689mg, Potassium 222g*

118. Bacon Veggie Casserole

Preparation time: 10 minutes

Cooking time: 30

minutes Servings: 12

INGREDIENTS

- *16 eggs*
- *¼ cup whole milk*
- *1 cup cooked, sliced bacon*
- *10 oz frozen, chopped spinach, thawed, drained*
- *2 cups chopped asparagus*
- *½ cup sundried tomatoes, chopped*
- *1 cup cheddar cheese, grated*
- *½ cup grated parmesan cheese*
- *½ cup whole milk ricotta*
- *¼ cup chopped white onion*
- *1 tsp minced garlic*
- *1 tsp sea salt*
- *½ tsp dried thyme*
- *½ tsp ground black pepper*

DIRECTIONS

1. *Preheat your air fryer to 350 degrees F and prepare a large baking dish with baking grease (make sure the pan will fit in your air fryer.*
2. *Whisk the eggs and milk in a large bowl.*
3. *Add the bacon, asparagus, tomatoes and spinach to the egg mix.*
4. *Add all the remaining ingredients, except the ricotta, and stir well.*
5. *Pour the egg and veggie mix into the prepared tray.*
6. *Dollop the ricotta around the pan, dispersing it evenly.*
7. *Bake in the air fryer for 30 minutes or until the eggs are completely set.*

NUTRITION: *Calories 349, Total Fat 22g, Saturated Fat 8g, Total Carbs 11g, Net Carbs 9g, Protein 20g, Sugar 3g, Fiber 2g, Sodium 689mg, Potassium 222g*

119. Broccoli and Bacon Fritters

Preparation time: 10 minutes

Cooking time: 30 minutes Servings: 4

INGREDIENTS

- *¾ cup almond flour*
- *7 Tbsp ground flaxseeds*
- *1 cup broccoli, fresh*
- *½ cup cooked, crumbled bacon*
- *4 ounces grated mozzarella cheese*
    - *2 eggs*
    - *2 tsp baking powder*
    - *1 tsp salt*
    - *¼ tsp ground black pepper*
    - *1 Tbsp olive oil*

DIRECTIONS

1. *Preheat your air fryer to 400 degrees F and prepare a large baking dish with foil.*
2. *Place the broccoli in a food processor along with the mozzarella, bacon, almond flour, 4 tablespoons of the flaxseeds and baking powder. Pulse until the mixture reaches a crumbly texture.*
3. *Add the eggs, salt and pepper and pulse until a dough forms.*
4. *Scoop the mix into bite sized balls, rolling them between your hands.*
5. *Roll the balls in the remaining flaxseeds and place on the prepared baking tray.*
6. *Drizzle with the olive oil and roll the balls around on the tray so the olive oil is coating the outside.*
7. *Place in the preheated air fryer and bake for 10 minutes or until nicely golden brown. Enjoy hot.*

NUTRITION: *Calories 278, Total Fat 26g, Saturated Fat 12g, Total Carbs 7g, Net Carbs 3g, Protein 21g, Sugar 1g, Fiber 4g, Sodium 1346mg, Potassium 190g*

120. Cauliflower and Bacon Fritters

Preparation time: 10 minutes

Cooking time: 30 minutes Servings: 4

INGREDIENTS

- *¾ cup almond flour*
- *7 Tbsp ground flaxseeds*
- *1 cup cauliflower, fresh*
- *½ cup cooked, crumbled bacon*
- *4 ounces grated mozzarella cheese*
- *2 eggs*
- *2 tsp baking powder*
- *1 tsp salt*
- *¼ tsp ground black pepper*
- *1 Tbsp olive oil*

DIRECTIONS

1. *Preheat your air fryer to 400 degrees F and prepare a large baking dish with foil.*
2. *Place the cauliflower in a food processor along with the mozzarella, bacon, almond flour, 4 tablespoons of the flaxseeds and baking powder. Pulse until the mixture reaches a crumbly texture.*
3. *Add the eggs, salt and pepper and pulse until a dough forms.*
4. *Scoop the mix into bite sized balls, rolling them between your hands.*
5. *Roll the balls in the remaining flaxseeds and place on the prepared baking tray.*
6. *Drizzle with the olive oil and roll the balls around on the tray so the olive oil is coating the outside.*
7. *Place in the preheated air fryer and bake for 10 minutes or until nicely golden brown. Enjoy hot.*

NUTRITION: *Calories 270, Total Fat 26g, Saturated Fat 12g, Total Carbs 6g, Net Carbs 4g, Protein 21g, Sugar 1g, Fiber 4g, Sodium 1207mg, Potassium 167g*

121. Mushroom and Bacon Fritters

Preparation time: 10 minutes

Cooking time: 30 minutes Servings: 4

INGREDIENTS

- *¾ cup almond flour*
- *7 Tbsp ground flaxseeds*
- *1 ½ cup chopped mushrooms, fresh*
- *½ cup cooked, crumbled bacon*
- *4 ounces grated mozzarella cheese*
- *2 eggs*
- *2 tsp baking powder*
- *1 tsp salt*
- *¼ tsp ground black pepper*
- *1 Tbsp olive oil*

DIRECTIONS

1. *Preheat your air fryer to 400 degrees F and prepare a large baking dish with foil.*
2. *Place the mushrooms in a food processor along with the mozzarella, bacon, almond flour, 4 tablespoons of the flaxseeds and baking powder. Pulse until the mixture reaches a crumbly texture.*
3. *Add the eggs, salt and pepper and pulse until a dough forms.*
4. *Scoop the mix into bite sized balls, rolling them between your hands.*
5. *Roll the balls in the remaining flaxseeds and place on the prepared baking tray.*
6. *Drizzle with the olive oil and roll the balls around on the tray so the olive oil is coating the outside.*
7. *Place in the preheated air fryer and bake for 10 minutes or until nicely golden brown. Enjoy hot.*

NUTRITION: *Calories 265, Total Fat 26g, Saturated Fat 12g, Total Carbs 6g, Net Carbs 2g, Protein 21g, Sugar 1g, Fiber 4g, Sodium 1300mg, Potassium 177g*

122. Cheesy Bacon Fritters

Preparation time: 10 minutes

Cooking time: 30 minutes Servings: 4

INGREDIENTS

- *¾ cup almond flour*
- *7 Tbsp ground flaxseeds*
- *1 cup cooked, crumbled bacon*
- *4 ounces grated mozzarella cheese*
- *½ cup grated parmesan*
- *2 eggs*
- *2 tsp baking powder*
- *1 tsp salt*
- *¼ tsp ground black pepper*
- *1 Tbsp olive oil*

DIRECTIONS

1. *Preheat your air fryer to 400 degrees F and prepare a large baking dish with foil.*
2. *Place the mozzarella, parmesan, bacon, almond flour, 4 tablespoons of the flaxseeds and baking powder. Pulse until the mixture reaches a crumbly texture.*
3. *Add the eggs, salt and pepper and pulse until a dough forms.*
4. *Scoop the mix into bite sized balls, rolling them between your hands.*
5. *Roll the balls in the remaining flaxseeds and place on the prepared baking tray.*
6. *Drizzle with the olive oil and roll the balls around on the tray so the olive oil is coating the outside.*
7. *Place in the preheated air fryer and bake*

   for 10 minutes or until nicely golden brown. Enjoy hot.

NUTRITION: *Calories 288, Total Fat 29g, Saturated Fat 15g, Total Carbs 7g, Net Carbs 3g, Protein 21g, Sugar 1g, Fiber 4g, Sodium 1368mg, Potassium 190g*

VEGAN & VEGETARIAN

123. Keto Pizza

Preparation time: 20 minutes

Cooking time: 20 minutes Servings: 3

INGREDIENTS

- *1 cup almond flour*
- *1 egg*
- *3 Tbsp water*
- *1 tsp minced garlic*
- *1 Tbsp fresh chopped basil*
- *4 Tbsp fresh grated parmesan*
- *¼ cup keto tomato sauce*
- *½ cup fresh diced mozzarella*

DIRECTIONS

1. *Preheat your air fryer to 375 degrees F and line the air fryer tray or baking pan with foil.*
2. *In a medium sized bowl, mix together the almond flour and water.*
3. *Add the egg and parmesan to the bowl and knead into a soft dough.*
4. *Place the dough on the prepared tray and press into a flat circle, about ¼ inch thick. Wet your hands if needed in order to make it easier to push the dough down.*
5. *Spread the tomato sauce over the dough and then top with the minced garlic, fresh basil and mozzarella.*
6. *Place in the preheated air fryer and bake for 18 minutes or until the cheese is melted and bubbling.*
7. *Slice and serve*

NUTRITION: *Calories 323, Total Fat 24g, Saturated Fat 12g, Total Carbs 11g, Net Carbs 8g, Protein 14g, Sugar 6g, Fiber 3g, Sodium 342mg, Potassium 98g*

Preparation time: 20 minutes Cooking time: 20 minutes Servings: 3

124. Extra Cheese Pizza

INGREDIENTS

- *1 cup almond flour*
- *1 egg*
- *3 Tbsp water*
- *1 tsp minced garlic*
- *1 Tbsp fresh chopped basil*
- *4 Tbsp fresh grated parmesan*
- *¼ cup keto tomato sauce*
- *½ cup fresh diced mozzarella*
- *½ cup shaved parmesan*
- *¼ cup shredded cheddar cheese* ***DIRECTIONS***

1. *Preheat your air fryer to 375 degrees F and line the air fryer tray or baking pan with foil.*
2. *In a medium sized bowl, mix together the almond flour and water.*
3. *Add the egg and parmesan to the bowl and knead into a soft dough.*
4. *Place the dough on the prepared tray and press into a flat circle, about ¼ inch thick. Wet your hands if needed in order to make it easier to push the dough down.*
5. *Spread the tomato sauce over the dough and then top with the minced garlic, fresh basil, shaved parmesan, cheddar, and mozzarella.*
6. *Place in the preheated air fryer and bake for 18 minutes or until the cheese is melted and bubbling.*
7. *Slice and serve*

NUTRITION: *Calories 419, Total Fat 36g, Saturated Fat 24g, Total Carbs 13g, Net Carbs 9g, Protein 19g, Sugar 8g, Fiber 4g, Sodium 452mg, Potassium 110g*

125. Roasted Squash Grits

Preparation time: 20 minutes

Cooking time: 23 minutes Servings: 4

INGREDIENTS

- *½ pound chopped butternut squash*
- *1 Tbsp minced garlic*
- *1 Tbsp fresh chopped rosemary*
- *½ cup chopped walnuts*
- *2 Tbsp olive oil*
- *2 cups chopped cauliflower florets*
- *1 cup heavy cream*
- *½ cup water*
- *1 cup shredded cheddar cheese*
- *2 Tbsp butter*
- *1 tsp salt*
- *¼ tsp ground black pepper*

DIRECTIONS

1. *Preheat your air fryer to 400 degrees F and line the air fryer tray or baking pan with foil.*
2. *Place the butternut squash, garlic, rosemary, olive oil and walnuts on the tray and toss to coat everything in the olive oil.*
3. *Place the tray in the air fryer and cook for 15 minutes.*
4. *While the squash is cooking, place the cauliflower in a blender or food processor and pulse until the cauliflower is like rice.*
5. *Place the cauliflower in a pot along with the water and cook over medium heat for 5 minutes.*
6. *Add the heavy cream and cook for another 3 minutes.*
7. *Stir in the cheese, butter, salt and pepper and mix to melt the cheese.*
8. *Divide between bowls and top with the roasted mushrooms. Enjoy hot!*

NUTRITION: *Calories 485, Total Fat 37g, Saturated Fat 8g, Total Carbs 18g, Net Carbs 12g, Protein 13g, Sugar 4g, Fiber 6g, Sodium 463mg, Potassium 163g*

126. Broccoli and Grits

Preparation time: 20 minutes

Cooking time: 23 minutes Servings: 4

INGREDIENTS

- *½ pound chopped broccoli florets*
- *1 Tbsp minced garlic*
- *1 Tbsp fresh chopped rosemary*
- *½ cup chopped pecans*
- *2 Tbsp olive oil*
- *2 cups chopped cauliflower florets*
- *1 cup heavy cream*
- *½ cup water*
- *1 cup shredded cheddar cheese*
- *2 Tbsp butter*
- *1 tsp salt*
- *¼ tsp ground black pepper*

DIRECTIONS

1. *Preheat your air fryer to 400 degrees F and line the air fryer tray or baking pan with foil.*
2. *Place the broccoli, garlic, rosemary, olive oil and pecans on the tray and toss to coat everything in the oil.*
3. *Place the tray in the air fryer and cook for 15 minutes.*
4. *While the broccoli is cooking, place the cauliflower in a blender or food processor and pulse until the cauliflower is like rice.*
5. *Place the cauliflower in a pot along with the water and cook over medium heat for 5 minutes.*
6. *Add the heavy cream and cook for another 3 minutes.*
7. *Stir in the cheese, butter, salt and pepper and mix to melt the cheese.*
8. *Divide between bowls and top with the roasted mushrooms. Enjoy hot!*

NUTRITION: *Calories 455, Total Fat 36g, Saturated Fat 8g, Total Carbs 17g, Net Carbs 11g, Protein 16g, Sugar 4g, Fiber 6g, Sodium 463mg, Potassium 163g*

127. Mug Lasagna

Preparation time: 5 minutes

Cooking time: 15 minutes Servings: 1

INGREDIENTS

- *½ large zucchini, sliced thinly*
- *3 Tbsp keto marinara sauce*
- *2 Tbsp ricotta, whole milk*
- *¼ cup fresh chopped mozzarella*

DIRECTIONS

1. *Preheat your air fryer to 400 degrees F.*
2. *Get an oven safe large ramekin or mug.*
3. *Lay some of the zucchini slices in the bottom of the cup.*
4. *Spread about 1 tablespoon of the ricotta on top of the zucchini then top with a tablespoon of the marinara sauce.*
5. *Layer more zucchini on top of the marinara and repeat the layering process until you have used all the zucchini,*

ricotta and marinara.

6. *Top with the mozzarella.*
7. *Place the lasagna in the oven and bake for 15 minutes or until the mozzarella is melted and bubbly. Enjoy hot*

NUTRITION: *Calories 318, Total Fat 24g, Saturated Fat 15g, Total Carbs 7g, Net Carbs 6g, Protein 20g, Sugar 3g, Fiber 1g, Sodium 562mg, Potassium 248g*

128. Mushroom Lunch Lasagna

Preparation time: 5 minutes

Cooking time: 15 minutes Servings: 1

INGREDIENTS

- *½ large zucchini, sliced thinly*
- *½ cup thinly sliced mushrooms*
- *3 Tbsp keto marinara sauce*
- *2 Tbsp ricotta, whole milk*
- *¼ cup fresh chopped mozzarella*

DIRECTIONS

1. *Preheat your air fryer to 400 degrees F.*
2. *Get an oven safe large ramekin or mug.*
3. *Lay some of the zucchini and mushroom slices in the bottom of the cup.*
4. *Spread about 1 tablespoon of the ricotta on top of the zucchini then top with a tablespoon of the marinara sauce.*
5. *Layer more zucchini and mushrooms on top of the marinara and repeat the layering process until you have used all the zucchini, mushrooms, ricotta and marinara.*
6. *Top with the mozzarella.*
7. *Place the lasagna in the oven and bake for 15 minutes or until the mozzarella is melted and bubbly. Enjoy hot*

NUTRITION: *Calories 343, Total Fat 24g, Saturated Fat 15g, Total Carbs 9g, Net Carbs 6g, Protein 20g, Sugar 4g, Fiber 2g, Sodium 562mg, Potassium 248g*

129. Eggplant Caprese Rollups

Preparation time: 5 minutes Cooking time: 8 minutes Servings: 8

INGREDIENTS

- *1 eggplant, sliced thinly lengthwise*
- *4 oz mozzarella cheese, sliced*
- *1 tomato, sliced*
- *2 Tbsp chopped fresh basil*
- *2 Tbsp olive oil*

DIRECTIONS

1. *Preheat your air fryer to 400 degrees F and prepare a large baking dish with foil.*
2. *Lay the eggplant slices out on a clean work surface.*
3. *Place a piece of tomato, cheese and a little basil on each eggplant slice and then roll up to enclose the filling.*
4. *Secure using a toothpick and then place the eggplant rolls on the prepared foil lined baking dish.*
5. *Drizzle with the olive oil and place in the air fryer to cook for 8 minutes. The eggplant should be lightly brown and the cheese melted. Serve warm.*

NUTRITION: *Calories 59, Total Fat 3g, Saturated Fat 1g, Total Carbs 4g, Net Carbs 3g, Protein 3g, Sugar 2g, Fiber 1g, Sodium 90mg, Potassium 178mg*

130. Eggplant Parmesan Rollups

Preparation time: 5 minutes Cooking time: 8 minutes Servings: 8

INGREDIENTS

- *1 eggplant, sliced thinly lengthwise*
- *4 oz grated parmesan*
- *1 tomato, sliced*
- *2 Tbsp chopped fresh basil*
- *2 Tbsp olive oil*

DIRECTIONS

1. *Preheat your air fryer to 400 degrees F and prepare a large baking dish with foil.*
2. *Lay the eggplant slices out on a clean work surface.*
3. *Place a piece of tomato, cheese and a little basil on each eggplant slice and then roll up to enclose the filling.*
4. *Secure using a toothpick and then place the eggplant rolls on the prepared foil lined baking dish.*
5. *Drizzle with the olive oil and place in the air fryer to cook for 8 minutes. The eggplant should be lightly brown and the cheese melted. Serve warm.*

NUTRITION: *Calories 57, Total Fat 3g, Saturated Fat 1g, Total Carbs 4g, Net Carbs 3g, Protein 3g, Sugar 2g, Fiber 1g, Sodium 90mg, Potassium 178mg*

131. Eggplant Zucchini Rollups

Preparation time: 5 minutes

Cooking time: 8 minutes Servings: 8

INGREDIENTS

- *1 eggplant, sliced thinly lengthwise*
- *4 oz mozzarella cheese, sliced*
- *1 zucchini, sliced lengthwise*
- *2 Tbsp chopped fresh basil*
- *2 Tbsp olive oil*

DIRECTIONS

1. *Preheat your air fryer to 400 degrees F and prepare a large baking dish with foil.*
2. *Lay the eggplant slices out on a clean work surface.*
3. *Place a piece of zucchini, cheese and a little basil on each eggplant slice and then roll up to enclose the filling.*
4. *Secure using a toothpick and then place the eggplant rolls on the prepared foil lined baking dish.*
5. *Drizzle with the olive oil and place in the air fryer to cook for 8 minutes. The eggplant should be lightly brown and the cheese melted. Serve warm.*

NUTRITION: *Calories 68, Total Fat 3g, Saturated Fat 1g, Total Carbs 5g, Net Carbs 4g, Protein 3g, Sugar 1g, Fiber 1g, Sodium 90mg, Potassium 178mg*

132. Zucchini Caprese Rollups

Preparation time: 5 minutes

Cooking time: 8 minutes

Servings: 8

INGREDIENTS

- *1 Zucchini, sliced thinly lengthwise*
- *4 oz mozzarella cheese, sliced*
- *1 tomato, sliced*
- *2 Tbsp chopped fresh basil*
- *2 Tbsp olive oil*

DIRECTIONS

1. *Preheat your air fryer to 400 degrees F and prepare a large baking dish with foil.*
2. *Lay the zucchini slices out on a clean work surface.*
3. *Place a piece of tomato, cheese and a little basil on each zucchini slice and then roll up to enclose the filling.*
4. *Secure using a toothpick and then place the eggplant rolls on the prepared foil lined baking dish.*
5. *Drizzle with the olive oil and place in the air fryer to cook for 8 minutes. The zucchini should be lightly brown and the cheese melted. Serve warm.*

NUTRITION: *Calories 61, Total Fat 3g, Saturated Fat 1g, Total Carbs 5g, Net Carbs 4g, Protein 3g, Sugar 3g, Fiber 1g, Sodium 90mg, Potassium 178mg*

133. Spicy Eggplant Rollups

Preparation time: 5 minutes

Cooking time: 8 minutes

Servings: 8

INGREDIENTS

- *1 eggplant, sliced thinly lengthwise*
- *4 oz parmesan cheese, sliced*
- *1 tomato, sliced*
- *2 Tbsp chopped fresh basil*
- *2 Tbsp olive oil*
- *1 tsp cayenne pepper*

DIRECTIONS

1. *Preheat your air fryer to 400 degrees F and prepare a large baking dish with foil.*
2. *Lay the eggplant slices out on a clean work surface.*
3. *Place a piece of tomato, cheese and a little basil on each eggplant slice and then roll up to enclose the filling.*
4. *Secure using a toothpick and then place the eggplant rolls on the prepared foil lined baking dish.*
5. *Drizzle with the olive oil, sprinkle with the cayenne and place in the air fryer to cook for 8 minutes. The eggplant should be lightly brown and the cheese melted. Serve warm.*

NUTRITION: *Calories 60, Total Fat 3g, Saturated Fat 1g, Total Carbs 4g, Net Carbs 3g, Protein 3g, Sugar 2g, Fiber 1g, Sodium 90mg,*

Potassium 178mg

134. Eggplant Tahini Rollups

Preparation time: 5 minutes

Cooking time: 8 minutes

Servings: 8

INGREDIENTS

- *1 eggplant, sliced thinly lengthwise*
- *4 oz mozzarella cheese, sliced*
- *¼ cup tahini paste*
- *2 Tbsp chopped fresh basil*
- *2 Tbsp olive oil*

DIRECTIONS

1. *Preheat your air fryer to 400 degrees F and prepare a large baking dish with foil.*
2. *Lay the eggplant slices out on a clean work surface.*
3. *Spread tahini on each eggplant then top with a slice of cheese and a little basil on each eggplant slice and then roll up to enclose the filling.*
4. *Secure using a toothpick and then place the eggplant rolls on the prepared foil lined baking dish.*
5. *Drizzle with the olive oil and place in the air fryer to cook for 8 minutes. The eggplant should be lightly brown and the cheese melted. Serve warm.*

NUTRITION: *Calories 68, Total Fat 4g, Saturated Fat 2g, Total Carbs 4g, Net Carbs 3g, Protein 4g, Sugar 2g, Fiber 1g, Sodium 105Mg, Potassium 178mg*

135. Lemon Eggplant Rollups

Preparation time: 5 minutes

Cooking time: 8 minutes

Servings: 8

INGREDIENTS

- *1 eggplant, sliced thinly lengthwise*
- *4 oz mozzarella cheese, sliced*
- *2 Tbsp chopped fresh basil*
- *2 Tbsp olive oil*
- *1 tsp lemon zest*

DIRECTIONS

1. *Preheat your air fryer to 400 degrees F and prepare a large baking dish with foil.*
2. *Lay the eggplant slices out on a clean work surface.*
3. *Place a piece of tomato, cheese and a little basil on each eggplant slice and then roll up to enclose the filling.*
4. *Secure using a toothpick and then place the eggplant rolls on the prepares foil lined baking dish.*
5. *Drizzle with the olive oil, sprinkle with the lemon zest and place in the air fryer to cook for 8 minutes. The eggplant should be lightly brown and the cheese melted. Serve warm.*

NUTRITION: *Calories 60, Total Fat 3g, Saturated Fat 1g, Total Carbs 4g, Net Carbs 3g, Protein 3g, Sugar 2g, Fiber 1g, Sodium 90mg, Potassium 178mg*

136. Tomato Lasagna

Preparation time: 5 minutes

Cooking time: 15 minutes Servings: 1

INGREDIENTS

- *½ large zucchini, sliced thinly*
- *½ cup sliced cherry tomatoes*
- *3 Tbsp keto marinara sauce*
- *2 Tbsp ricotta, whole milk*
- *¼ cup fresh chopped mozzarella*

DIRECTIONS

1. *Preheat your air fryer to 400 degrees F.*
2. *Get an oven safe large ramekin or mug.*
3. *Lay some of the zucchini slices in the bottom of the cup and top with a few tomato slices.*
4. *Spread about 1 tablespoon of the ricotta on top of the zucchini and tomatoes then top with a tablespoon of the marinara sauce.*
5. *Layer more zucchini and tomatoes on top of the marinara and repeat the layering process until you have used all the zucchini, tomatoes, ricotta and marinara.*
6. *Top with the mozzarella.*
7. *Place the lasagna in the oven and bake for 15 minutes or until the mozzarella is melted and bubbly. Enjoy hot*

NUTRITION: *Calories 345, Total Fat 24g, Saturated Fat 15g, Total Carbs 10g, Net Carbs 8g, Protein 20g, Sugar 4g, Fiber 1g, Sodium 562mg, Potassium 248g*

137. Spicy Egg Salad

Preparation time: 5 minutes

Cooking time: 16 minutes Servings: 6

INGREDIENTS

- *6 Tbsp Mayonnaise*
- *8 Large Eggs*
- *2 Tbsp apple cider vinegar*
- *1 tsp ground black pepper*
- *1 tsp salt*
- *¼ tsp paprika*
- *1 tsp cayenne pepper, ground*

DIRECTIONS

1. *Preheat your air fryer to 250 degrees F.*
2. *Place a wire rack in the air fryer and place the eggs on top of the rack.*
3. *Cook for 16 minutes then remove the eggs and place them directly into an ice water bath to cool and stop the cooking process.*
4. *Peel the eggs and place in a large bowl.*
5. *Mash the eggs with a fork.*
6. *Add in the mayonnaise, cider vinegar, pepper, cayenne, paprika and salt*

NUTRITION: *Calories 189, Total Fat 12g, Saturated Fat 6g, Total Carbs 2g, Net Carbs 1g, Protein 12g, Sugar 0g, Fiber 1g, Sodium 458mg, Potassium 289g*

138. Roasted Brussels Sprout Salad

Preparation time: 7 minutes

Cooking time: 15 minutes Servings: 4

INGREDIENTS

- *1 pound Brussel sprouts, sliced in quarters*
- *1 tsp minced, fresh rosemary*
- *¼ cup olive oil*
- *1 Tbsp apple cider vinegar*
- *2 Tbsp lemon juice*
- *½ tsp Dijon mustard*
- *½ tsp kosher salt*

DIRECTIONS

1. *Preheat your air fryer to 450 degrees F and line the air fryer tray or baking pan with foil.*
2. *Toss the Brussels sprouts with the rosemary and olive oil and place on the prepared tray.*
3. *Roast in the air fryer for 15 minutes.*
4. *Place the hot, roasted sprouts in a large bowl and add the remaining ingredients to make a dressing. Toss well and serve hot or cold.*

NUTRITION: *Calories 157, Total Fat 14g, Saturated Fat 2g, Total Carbs 9g, Net Carbs 6g, Protein 3g, Sugar 2g, Fiber 3g, Sodium 27mg, Potassium 509g*

139. Spicy Pepper Lasagna

Preparation time: 5 minutes

Cooking time: 15 minutes Servings: 1

INGREDIENTS

- *½ large zucchini, sliced thinly*
- *¼ cup chopped red bell peppers*
- *3 Tbsp keto marinara sauce*
- *2 Tbsp ricotta, whole milk*
- *¼ cup fresh chopped mozzarella*

DIRECTIONS

1. *Preheat your air fryer to 400 degrees F.*
2. *Get an oven safe large ramekin or mug.*
3. *Lay some of the zucchini slices and chopped bell peppers in the bottom of the cup.*
4. *Spread about 1 tablespoon of the ricotta on top of the zucchini then top with a tablespoon of the marinara sauce.*
5. *Layer more zucchini and peppers on top of the marinara and repeat the layering process until you have used all the zucchini, peppers ricotta and marinara.*
6. *Top with the mozzarella.*
7. *Place the lasagna in the oven and bake for 15 minutes or until the mozzarella is melted and bubbly. Enjoy hot*

NUTRITION: *Calories 325, Total Fat 24g, Saturated Fat 15g, Total Carbs 9g, Net Carbs 7g, Protein 20g, Sugar 4g, Fiber 2g, Sodium 573mg, Potassium 249g*

VEGETABLES

140. Orange Mango Salad

Preparation time: 5 minutes

Cooking time: 8 minutes Servings: 4

INGREDIENTS

- *1 cup mango, peeled and cubed 1 cup baby spinach*
- *1 cup cherry tomatoes, halved*
- *1 cup oranges, peeled and cut into segments 1 tablespoon olive oil*
- *1 tablespoon balsamic vinegar 2 teaspoons orange zest, grated A handful parsley, chopped*

DIRECTIONS

1. *In the air fryer's pan, mix the mango with the spinach and the other ingredients, toss and cook at 350 degrees F for 8 minutes.*
2. *Divide into bowls and serve.* NUTRITION: *Calories 151, Fat 6, Fiber 6, Carbs 11, Protein 5*

141. Avocado Salad

Preparation time: 5 minutes

Cooking time: 5 minutes Servings: 4

INGREDIENTS

- *red onion, sliced*
- *cups avocado, peeled, pitted and cubed 1 cup cherry tomatoes, halved*
- *2 tablespoons avocado oil Juice of 1 lime*
- *Salt and black pepper to the taste 1 cup walnuts, chopped*
- *1 tablespoon chives, chopped*

DIRECTIONS

In your air fryer, mix the avocado with the tomatoes and the other ingredients, toss, cook at 400 degrees F for 5 minutes, divide into bowls and serve.

NUTRITION: ***Calories 151, Fat 4, Fiber 6,***

Carbs 9,
Protein 4

142. Tomato and Shrimp Salad

Preparation time: 6 minutes

Cooking time: 6

minutes Servings: 4

INGREDIENTS

- *1 pound cherry tomatoes, halved*
- *½ pound shrimp, peeled and deveined Juice of 1 lime*
- *1 cup baby kale*
- *2 green onions, chopped 2 tomatoes, cubed*
- *jalapeno pepper, chopped 1 tablespoon olive oil*
- *teaspoons chili powder*
- *Salt and black pepper to the taste*

DIRECTIONS

1. *In a pan that fits your air fryer, mix the tomatoes with the shrimp, oil and the other ingredients, toss, introduce the pan in the fryer and cook at 400 degrees F for 6 minutes.*
2. *Divide the mix into bowls and serve.* NUTRITION: *Calories 200, Fat 4,*

Fiber 7, Carbs
12, Protein 6

143. Bell Peppers Salad

Preparation time: 10 minutes

Cooking time: 15 minutes Servings: 4

INGREDIENTS

- *2 red bell peppers, cut into strips*
- *2 green bell peppers, cut into strips 2 orange bell peppers, cut into strips 1 cup cherry tomatoes, halved*
- *cup baby spinach Juice of 1 lime*
- *tablespoons olive oil*
- *Salt and black pepper to the taste*

DIRECTIONS

1. *In a pan that fits your air fryer, mix the peppers with the tomatoes and the other ingredients, toss, introduce the pan in the fryer and cook at 360 degrees F for 15 minutes.*
2. *Divide into bowls and serve.* NUTRITION: *Calories 161, Fat 7, Fiber*

6, Carbs

12, Protein 7

144. Garlic Carrots and Spinach Salad

Preparation time: 10 minutes

Cooking time: 15 minutes Servings: 4

INGREDIENTS

- *1 pound baby carrots, peeled and sliced 1 cup baby spinach*
- *1 cup corn*
- *Juice of ½ lemon*
- *1 tablespoon olive oil 6 garlic cloves, minced*
- *1 tablespoon balsamic vinegar Salt and black pepper to the taste*

DIRECTIONS

1. *In the air fryer's pan, mix the carrots with the spinach and the other ingredients, toss and cook at 380 degrees F for 15 minutes.*
2. *Divide into bowls and serve.*

145. Sprouts and Pomegranate Mix

Preparation time: 5 minutes

Cooking time: 10 minutes Servings: 4

INGREDIENTS

- *1 pound Brussels sprouts, trimmed and halved*
- *1 cup pomegranate seeds 1 cup baby spinach*
- *tablespoon avocado oil*
- *tablespoons balsamic vinegar 1 teaspoon chili powder*
- *Salt and black pepper to the taste*

DIRECTIONS

1. *In the air fryer's pan, mix the sprouts with the pomegranate seeds and the other ingredients, toss and cook at 380 degrees F for 10 minutes.*
2. *Divide into bowls and serve.* NUTRITION: *Calories 141, Fat 3, Fiber 4,*

Carbs

11, Protein 4

146. Cauliflower and Pomegranate Mix

Preparation time: 6 minutes

Cooking time: 12 minutes Servings: 4

- *1 pound cauliflower florets 1 cup pomegranate seeds 1 tablespoon lime juice*
- *1 tablespoon orange juice 1 tablespoon olive oil*
- *Salt and black pepper to the taste 2 tablespoons chives, chopped*

DIRECTIONS

1. *In your air fryer's pan, mix the cauliflower with the pomegranate seeds and the other ingredients, toss, and cook at 400 degrees F for 12 minutes.*
2. *Divide into bowls and serve.* NUTRITION: *Calories 200, Fat 7, Fiber*

5, Carbs

17, Protein 7

147. Potato Salad

Preparation time: 4 minutes

Cooking time: 25 minutes Servings: 4

INGREDIENTS

- *1 pound sweet potatoes, peeled and cut into wedges*
- *1 cup baby spinach*
- *1 cup cherry tomatoes, halved*
- *1 cup black olives, pitted and halved 1 tablespoon olive oil*
- *1 teaspoon hot paprika 1 tablespoon lime juice*
- *Salt and black pepper to the taste*

DIRECTIONS

1. *In your air fryer, combine the potatoes with the spinach and the other ingredients, toss and cook at 400 degrees F for 25 minutes.*
2. *Divide into bowls and serve hot.* NUTRITION: *Calories 151, Fat 4,*

Fiber 7, Carbs
12, Protein 6

148. Baby Potatoes Mix

Preparation time: 10 minutes

Cooking time: 20 minutes Servings: 4

INGREDIENTS

- *1 pound baby potatoes, peeled and halved 1 cup green beans, trimmed and halved*
- *cup corn*
- *tablespoons avocado oil Juice of 1 lime*
- *Salt and black pepper to the taste 3 garlic cloves, minced*
  - *½ teaspoon rosemary, dried 1 teaspoon turmeric powder 1 tablespoon dill, chopped*

DIRECTIONS

1. *In the air fryer's pan, mix the potatoes with the green beans and the other ingredients, toss and cook at 400 degrees F for 20 minutes.*
2. *Divide between plates and serve.* NUTRITION: *Calories 171, Fat 5, Fiber 6, Carbs 15, Protein 8*

149. Cabbage Salad

Preparation time: 10 minutes

Cooking time: 15 minutes Servings: 4

INGREDIENTS

- *1 pound red cabbage, shredded 1 red onion, sliced*
- *1 cup carrots, peeled and shredded Juice of 1 lime*
- *tablespoon olive oil*
- *¼ teaspoon sweet paprika*
- *Salt and black pepper to the taste 1 tablespoon dill, chopped*

DIRECTIONS

1. *In a pan that fits your air fryer, mix the cabbage with the onion and the other ingredients , toss, introduce the pan in the fryer and cook at 400 degrees F for 15 minutes.*
2. *Divide into bowls and serve.* NUTRITION: *Calories 154, Fat 4, Fiber 4, Carbs 12, Protein 5*

150. Cabbage and Pomegranate Mix

Preparation time: 10 minutes

Cooking time: 12 minutes Servings: 4

INGREDIENTS

- *1 pound green cabbage, shredded*
- *¼ cup butter, melted*
- *1 cup pomegranate seeds*
- *1 tablespoon chives, chopped*
- *A pinch of salt and black pepper 1 tablespoon sweet paprika*
- *1 tablespoon dill, chopped*

DIRECTIONS

1. *In a pan that fits your air fryer, mix the cabbage with the butter and the other ingredients, toss, introduce the pan in the fryer and cook at 380 degrees F for 12 minutes.*
2. *Divide everything into bowls and serve.* NUTRITION: *Calories 181, Fat 4, Fiber 6, Carbs 15, Protein 5*

151. Kale Salad

Preparation time: 4 minutes

Cooking time: 15 minutes Servings: 4

INGREDIENTS

- *1 pound baby kale 1 cup corn*
- *1 cup cherry tomatoes, halved 1 tablespoon olive oil*
- *Juice of 1 lime*
- *Salt and black pepper to the taste*
- *½ cup spring onions, chopped*

DIRECTIONS

1. *In a pan that fits your air fryer, mix the kale with the corn and the other ingredients, toss, introduce the pan in the fryer and cook at 350 degrees F for 15 minutes.*
2. *Divide the salad into bowls and serve.* **NUTRITION:** *Calories 151, Fat 4, Fiber 5, Carbs 15, Protein 6*

152. Spicy Green Beans Mix

Preparation time: 5 minutes

Cooking time: 15 minutes Servings: 4

INGREDIENTS

- *1 pound green beans, trimmed and halved 2 red chilies, minced*
- *1 tablespoon lemon juice 1 tablespoon olive oil*
- *1 teaspoon hot paprika*
- *A pinch of salt and black pepper*
- *tablespoons chives, chopped*

DIRECTIONS

1. *In a pan that fits your air fryer, mix the green beans with the chilies and the other ingredients, toss, introduce in the fryer and cook at 320 degrees F for 15 minutes.*
2. *Divide between plates and serve right away.*

NUTRITION: ***Calories 124, Fat 6, Fiber 6, Carbs***

16, Protein 7

153. Roast Celeriac

Preparation time: 10 minutes

Cooking time: 15 minutes Servings: 4

INGREDIENTS

- *2 cups celeriac, peeled and roughly cubed 2 tablespoons olive oil*
- *Juice of 1 lime*
- *A pinch of salt and black pepper*
- *½ tablespoon chives, chopped*

DIRECTIONS

1. *In the air fryer, combine the celeriac with the oil and the other ingredients, toss and cook at 380 degrees F for 15 minutes.*
2. *Divide between plates and serve.* NUTRITION: *Calories 124, Fat 1, Fiber 4, Carbs 6, Protein 6*

154. Maple Corn

Preparation time: 5 minutes

Cooking time: 15 minutes Servings: 4

INGREDIENTS

- *2 cups corn*
- *1 tablespoon avocado oil Juice of 1 lime*
- *1 tablespoon maple syrup*
- *Salt and black pepper to the taste*
- *1 tablespoon chives, chopped*

DIRECTIONS

1. *In the air fryer, combine the corn with the oil and the other ingredients, toss and cook at 390 degrees F for 15 minutes.*
2. *Divide the mix between plates and serve.* NUTRITION: *Calories 100, Fat 2, Fiber 3, Carbs 8,*

Protein 3

155. Dill Mango and Corn

Preparation time: 5 minutes

Cooking time: 12 minutes Servings: 4

INGREDIENTS

- *2 cups corn*
- *1 cup mango, peeled and cubed*
- *1 cup baby spinach*
- *1 tablespoon olive oil Juice of 1 lime*
- *Salt and black pepper to the taste*
- *2 tablespoon dill, chopped*

DIRECTIONS

1. *In your air fryer, combine the corn with the mango and the other ingredients, toss and cook at 390 degrees F for 12 minutes.*
2. *Divide the mix into bowls and serve.* NUTRITION: *Calories 100, Fat 2, Fiber 5, Carbs 9, Protein 6*

156. Spring Onions and Pasta

Preparation time: 10 minutes

Cooking time: 15 minutes

Servings: 4

INGREDIENTS

- *2 tablespoons butter, melted 2 cups small pasta*
- *½ cup spring onions, chopped 1 cup heavy cream*
- *1 cup chicken stock*
- *Salt and black pepper to the taste 1 tablespoon parmesan, grated*
- *1 tablespoon chives, chopped*

DIRECTIONS

1. *Grease A Baking Dish That Fits Your Air Fryer With The Butter, Combine All The Ingredients Inside, Introduce The Dish In The Fryer And Cook At 390 Degrees F For 15 Minutes.*
2. *Divide Everything Between Plates And Serve.*

NUTRITION: ***Calories 151, Fat 6, Fiber 5, Carbs***

12, Protein 4

157. Mustard Greens and Spinach

Preparation time: 10 minutes

Cooking time: 12 minutes Servings: 4

INGREDIENTS

- *1 pound mustard greens, torn*
- *½ pound spinach, torn*
- *1 cup cherry tomatoes, halved*
- *1 cup black olives, pitted and halved 1 teaspoon sweet paprika*
    - *A drizzle of olive oil*
    - *Salt and black pepper to the taste*
    - *½ cup veggie stock*

DIRECTIONS

1. *In a pan that fits your air fryer, mix the mustard greens with the spinach and the other ingredients, toss, introduce the pan in the fryer and cook at 300 degrees F for 12 minutes.*
2. *Divide everything between plates and serve.*

NUTRITION: ***Calories 161, Fat 4, Fiber 5, Carbs***

14, Protein 3

158. Balsamic Spinach

Preparation time: 10 minutes

Cooking time: 12 minutes

Servings: 4

INGREDIENTS

- *1 pound spinach*
- *2 tablespoons olive oil*
- *½ cup chicken stock*
- *1 teaspoon coriander, ground 1 teaspoon rosemary, dried*
- *1 cup cherry tomatoes, halved Salt and black pepper to the taste 1 tablespoon balsamic vinegar*

DIRECTIONS

1. *In a pan that fits your air fryer, mix the spinach with the oil and the other ingredients, toss, introduce in the fryer and cook at 260 degrees F for 12 minutes.*
2. *Divide everything into bowls and serve.* NUTRITION: *Calories 151, Fat 2,*

Fiber 4, Carbs

14, Protein 4

159. Endives and Pomegranate Mix

Preparation time: 10 minutes

Cooking time: 12 minutes Servings: 4

INGREDIENTS

- *4 endives, trimmed and shredded 1 cup pomegranate seeds*
- *1 cup baby spinach*
- *Salt and black pepper to the taste*
- *1 tablespoon lime juice 1 tablespoon olive*

  oil

- *1 teaspoon chili powder*

DIRECTIONS

1. *In air fryer, mix the endives with the pomegranate seeds and the other ingredients, toss, cook at 360 degrees F for 12 minutes, divide between plates and serve.*

NUTRITION: ***Calories 100, Fat 3, Fiber 4,***

Carbs 8,
Protein 4

160. Nutmeg Endives

Preparation time: 10 minutes

Cooking time: 12 minutes Servings: 4

INGREDIENTS

- *4 endives, trimmed and halved 1 teaspoon nutmeg, ground*
- *1 teaspoon sweet paprika 2 tablespoons avocado oil Juice of 1 lime*
- *Salt and black pepper to the taste*

DIRECTIONS

1. *Put the endives in your air fryer's basket, add the rest of the ingredients, toss and cook at 360 degrees F for 12 minutes.*
2. *Divide the mix between plates and serve.* NUTRITION: *Calories 151, Fat 6,*

Fiber 8, Carbs
14, Protein 6

161. Leeks and Grapes Mix

Preparation time: 5 minutes

Cooking time: 15 minutes Servings: 4

INGREDIENTS

- *4 leeks, sliced*
- *1 cup grapes*
- *1 tablespoon avocado oil Juice of 1 lime*
- *1 avocado, peeled, pitted and cubed Salt and black pepper to the taste*
- *1 tablespoon chives, chopped*

DIRECTIONS

1. *In the air fryer's pan, combine the leeks with the grapes and the other ingredients, toss and cook at 360 degrees F for 15 minutes.*
2. *Divide into bowls and serve.* NUTRITION: *Calories 108, Fat 6, Fiber 1.7, Carbs 13.2, Protein 1.7*

162. Rice, Mushrooms and Pomegranate Mix

Preparation time: 10 minutes

Cooking time: 25 minutes Servings: 4

INGREDIENTS

- *1 cup white rice*
- *½ cup pomegranate seeds*
- *cup white mushrooms, sliced 1 tablespoon olive oil*
- *cups chicken stock*
- *Salt and black pepper to the taste*
- *½ teaspoon chili powder*
- *1 tablespoon cilantro, chopped*

DIRECTIONS

1. *In your air fryer's pan, combine the rice with the pomegranate seeds and the other ingredients, toss, and cook at 360 degrees F for 25 minutes.*
2. *Divide the mix between plates and serve.* NUTRITION: *Calories 182, Fat 1.6, Fiber 2, Carbs 37.5, Protein 4.3*

163. Sprouts and Leeks

Preparation time: 5 minutes

Cooking time: 20 minutes Servings: 4

INGREDIENTS

- *1 pound Brussels sprouts, trimmed and halved*
- *2 leeks, sliced*
- *½ cup veggie stock*
- *2 tablespoons chives, chopped 1 tablespoon avocado oil*
- *1 teaspoon chili powder*
- *1 teaspoon turmeric powder*
- *Salt and black pepper to the taste*

DIRECTIONS

1. *In the air fryer's pan, mix the sprouts with the leeks and the other ingredients, toss and cook everything for 20 minutes at 380 degrees F.*
2. *Divide the mix between plates and serve.* NUTRITION: *Calories 200, Fat 15.1, Fiber 5, Carbs 15.2, Protein 5.1*

164. Green Beans and Avocado Mix

Preparation time: 10 minutes

Cooking time: 20 minutes Servings: 4

INGREDIENTS

- *2 pounds green beans, trimmed and halved 1 cup avocado, peeled, pitted and cubed*
- *1 cup mango, peeled and cubed 1 tablespoon olive oil*
- *1 teaspoon chili powder*
- *1 tablespoon lemon zest, grated 1 tablespoon lemon juice*
- *Salt and black pepper to the taste*

DIRECTIONS

1. *In the air fryer's pan, combine the green beans with the avocado and the other ingredients, toss and cook at 360 degrees F for 20 minutes.*
2. *Divide between plates and serve.* NUTRITION: *Calories 108, Fat 4,*

Fiber 8, Carbs
17.4, Protein 4.4

165. Curry Green Beans

Preparation time: 5 minutes

Cooking time: 20 minutes Servings: 4

INGREDIENTS

- *1 pound green beans, trimmed and halved 1 tablespoon green curry paste*
- *1 tablespoons butter, melted 1 teaspoon curry powder*
- *¼ cup veggie stock*
- *1 teaspoon sweet paprika*
- *A pinch of salt and black pepper 1 tablespoon chives, chopped*

DIRECTIONS

1. *In your air fryer's pan, mix the green beans with the curry paste and the other ingredients, toss and cook at 360 degrees F for 20 minutes.*
2. *Divide everything between plates and serve.*

NUTRITION: ***Calories 194, Fat 4, Fiber 4, Carbs***

8.4, Protein 7

166. Zucchini and Avocado Mix

Preparation time: 5 minutes Cooking time: 15 minutes Servings: 4

INGREDIENTS

- *1 pound zucchinis, roughly cubed*
- *1 cup avocado, peeled, pitted and cubed 1 tablespoon olive oil*
- *Juice of 1 lime*
- *1 teaspoon nutmeg, ground*
- *Salt and black pepper to the taste*
- *½ teaspoon garlic powder*
- *1 tablespoon chives, chopped*

DIRECTIONS

1. *In the air fryer's pan, mix the zucchinis with the avocado and the other ingredients, toss and cook at 360 degrees F for 15 minutes.*
2. *Divide between plates and serve.* NUTRITION: *Calories 210, Fat 5, Fiber 7, Carbs 12, Protein 5*

167. Spicy Tomatoes

Preparation time: 5 minutes

Cooking time: 15 minutes Servings: 4

INGREDIENTS

- *1 pound cherry tomatoes, halved 1 teaspoon chili powder*
- *1 teaspoon hot paprika*
- *1 jalapenos, chopped Juice of 1 lime*
- *2 tablespoon olive oil 2 garlic cloves, minced*
- *Salt and black pepper to the taste*

DIRECTIONS

1. *In the air fryer's pan, combine the tomatoes with the chili powder and the other ingredients, toss and cook at 350 degrees F for 15 minutes.*
2. *Divide between plates and serve.* NUTRITION: *Calories 174, Fat 5, Fiber 7, Carbs 11, Protein 4*

168. Tarragon Brussels Sprouts

Preparation time: 5 minutes

Cooking time: 20 minutes Servings: 4

INGREDIENTS

- *2 pounds Brussels sprouts, trimmed and halved*
- *1 teaspoon chili powder*
- *1 teaspoon cumin, ground*
- *1 tablespoon tarragon, chopped 2 tablespoons avocado oil*
- *1 teaspoon sweet paprika*
- *Salt and black pepper to the taste 1 tablespoon dill, chopped*

DIRECTIONS

1. *In the air fryer's basket, combine the sprouts*
2. *with the chili powder and the other ingredients, toss and cook at 360 degrees F for 20 minutes.*
3. *Divide between plates and serve.* NUTRITION: *Calories 214, Fat 5, Fiber 8, Carbs 12, Protein 5*

DESSERTS

169. Strawberry Fudge Brownies

Preparation time: 15 minutes

Cooking time: 20 minutes Servings: 16

INGREDIENTS

- *½ cup melted butter 2/3 cup swerve*
- *½ tsp vanilla extract*
- *room temperature eggs*
- *½ cup almond flour*
- *1/3 cup unsweetened cocoa powder 1 Tbsp plain, unsweetened gelatin*
- *½ tsp salt*
- *½ tsp baking powder*
- *¼ cup water*
- *½ cup fresh chopped strawberries*

DIRECTIONS

1. *Preheat your air fryer to 325 degrees F and grease an 8x8 inch square baking pan.*
2. *Combine the melted butter, vanilla extract, swerve, and melted butter in a bowl and whisk together well.*
3. *Add the cocoa powder, almond flour, baking powder, gelatin, and salt and whisk again until smooth.*
4. *Add the water and stir again. Fold in the strawberries*
5. *Pour the batter into the greased baking pan and place in the preheated air fryer. Bake for 15 minutes. The center will seem a little wet while the edges will be more firm- this is perfect.*
6. *Let the brownies cool in the pan before slicing and serving.*

NUTRITION: *Calories 193, Total Fat 10g, Saturated Fat 4g, Total Carbs 11g, Net Carbs 6g, Protein 3g, Sugar 5g, Fiber 5g, Sodium 283mg, Potassium 412g*

170. Cheesecake Fudge Brownies

Preparation time: 15 minutes

Cooking time: 20 minutes Servings: 16

INGREDIENTS

- *½ cup cream cheese, softened 3 Tbsp erythritol sweetener*
- *½ cup melted butter 2/3 cup swerve*
- *½ tsp vanilla extract*
- *room temperature eggs*
- *½ cup almond flour*
- *1/3 cup unsweetened cocoa powder 1 Tbsp plain, unsweetened gelatin*
- *½ tsp salt*
- *½ tsp baking powder*
- *¼ cup water*

DIRECTIONS

1. *Preheat your air fryer to 325 degrees F and grease an 8x8 inch square baking pan.*
2. *In a small bowl, mic the cream cheese and erythritol sweetener together. Set aside.*
3. *Combine the melted butter, vanilla extract, swerve, and melted butter in a bowl and whisk together well.*
4. *Add the cocoa powder, almond flour, baking powder, gelatin, and salt and whisk again until smooth.*
5. *Add the water and stir again.*
6. *Pour the batter into the greased baking pan and swirl in the cream cheese mix.*
7. *Place the pan in the preheated air fryer. Bake for 15 minutes. The center will seem a little wet while the edges will be more firm- this is perfect.*
8. *Let the brownies cool in the pan before slicing and serving.*

NUTRITION: *Calories 215, Total Fat 18g, Saturated Fat 5g, Total Carbs 6g, Net Carbs 3g, Protein 3g, Sugar 2g, Fiber 3g, Sodium 283mg, Potassium 316g*

171. Chocolate Chip Cookies

Preparation time: 10 minutes

Cooking time: 9 minutes

Servings: 12

INGREDIENTS

- *½ cup butter, melted*
- *¾ cup erythritol*
- *1 tsp vanilla extract 1 egg*
  - *1 ½ cups almond flour*
  - *½ tsp salt*
  - *½ tsp baking powder*
  - *¾ cup sugar free chocolate chips*

DIRECTIONS

1. *Preheat your air fryer to 330 degrees F and prepare your air fryer tray with a piece of parchment.*
2. *Beat the melted butter and erythritol together in a large bowl.*
3. *Add the eggs and vanilla and mix until the batter comes together.*
4. *Add the salt, baking powder and almond flour and mix until a nice, smooth batter forms.*
5. *Fold in the chocolate chips then scoop the cookie dough onto the prepared sheet tray. You will want to leave about 2 inches between the cookie dough scoops as the dough will spread slightly. If needed, you can bake the cookies in batches.*
6. *Bake the cookies in the air fryer for 8-9 minutes or until golden brown on the edges.*
7. *Let cool on the sheet tray for 5 minutes before removing and enjoying!*

NUTRITION: *Calories 168, Total Fat 18g, Saturated Fat 6g, Total Carbs 2g, Net Carbs 1g, Protein 4g, Sugar 1g, Fiber 1g, Sodium 342mg, Potassium 110g*

172. Butter Cookies

Preparation time: 10 minutes

Cooking time: 9 minutes Servings: 12

INGREDIENTS

- *½ cup butter, melted*
- *¾ cup erythritol*
- *1 tsp vanilla extract 1 egg*
- *1 ½ cups almond flour*
- *¼ tsp xanthan gum*
- *½ tsp salt*
- *½ tsp baking powder*

DIRECTIONS

1. *Preheat your air fryer to 330 degrees F and prepare your air fryer tray with a piece of parchment.*
2. *Beat the melted butter and erythritol*

   together in a large bowl.
3. *Add the eggs and vanilla and mix until the batter comes together.*
4. *Add the salt, baking powder, xanthan gum and almond flour and mix until a nice, smooth batter forms.*
5. *Scoop the cookie dough onto the prepared sheet tray. You will want to leave about 2*
6. *inches between the cookie dough scoops as the dough will spread slightly. If needed, you can bake the cookies in batches.*
7. *Bake the cookies in the air fryer for 8-9 minutes or until golden brown on the edges.*
8. *Let cool on the sheet tray for 5 minutes before removing and enjoying!*

NUTRITION: *Calories 110, Total Fat 12g, Saturated Fat 3g, Total Carbs 1g, Net Carbs 0g, Protein 3g, Sugar 0g, Fiber 1g, Sodium 342mg, Potassium 46mg*

173. Walnut Cookies

Preparation time: 10 minutes Cooking time: 9 minutes Servings: 12

INGREDIENTS

- *½ cup butter, melted*
- *¾ cup erythritol*
- *1 tsp vanilla extract 1 egg*
- *1 ½ cups almond flour*
- *½ tsp salt*
- *½ tsp baking powder*
- *¾ cup chopped walnuts*

DIRECTIONS

1. *Preheat your air fryer to 330 degrees F and prepare your air fryer tray with a piece of parchment.*
2. *Beat the melted butter and erythritol together in a large bowl.*
3. *Add the eggs and vanilla and mix until the batter comes together.*
4. *Add the salt, baking powder and almond flour and mix until a nice, smooth batter forms.*
5. *Fold in the walnuts then scoop the cookie dough onto the prepared sheet tray. You will want to leave about 2 inches between the cookie dough scoops as the dough will*

spread slightly. If needed, you can bake the cookies in batches.

6. *Bake the cookies in the air fryer for 8-9 minutes or until golden brown on the edges.*
7. *Let cool on the sheet tray for 5 minutes before removing and enjoying!*

NUTRITION: *Calories 174, Total Fat 18g, Saturated Fat 6g, Total Carbs 2g, Net Carbs 1g, Protein 7g, Sugar 1g, Fiber 1g, Sodium 342mg, Potassium 178g*

174. Coconut Cookies

Preparation time: 10 minutes

Cooking time: 9 minutes Servings: 12

INGREDIENTS

- *½ cup butter, melted*
- *¾ cup erythritol*
- *1 tsp vanilla extract 1 egg*
- *1 cup almond flour*
- *½ cup coconut flour*
- *½ tsp salt*
- *½ tsp baking powder*
- *½ cup unsweetened coconut flakes*

DIRECTIONS

1. *Preheat your air fryer to 330 degrees F and prepare your air fryer tray with a piece of parchment.*
2. *Beat the melted butter and erythritol together in a large bowl.*
3. *Add the eggs and vanilla and mix until the batter comes together.*
4. *Add the salt, baking powder coconut flour and almond flour and mix until a nice, smooth batter forms.*
5. *Fold in the coconut flakes then scoop the cookie dough onto the prepared sheet tray. You will want to leave about 2 inches between the cookie dough scoops as the dough will spread slightly. If needed, you can bake the cookies in batches.*
6. *Bake the cookies in the air fryer for 8-9 minutes or until golden brown on the edges.*
7. *Let cool on the sheet tray for 5 minutes before removing and enjoying!*

NUTRITION: ***Calories 178, Total Fat 16g,***

Saturated Fat 7g, Total Carbs 7g, Net Carbs 4g, Protein 5g, Sugar 3g, Fiber 3g, Sodium 342mg, Potassium 278g

175. Almond Cookies

Preparation time: 10 minutes

Cooking time: 9 minutes Servings: 12

INGREDIENTS

- *½ cup butter, melted*
- *¾ cup erythritol*
- *1 tsp almond extract 1 egg*
- *1 ½ cups almond flour*
- *½ tsp salt*
- *½ tsp baking powder*
- *¾ cup chopped almonds*

DIRECTIONS

1. *Preheat your air fryer to 330 degrees F and prepare your air fryer tray with a piece of parchment.*
2. *Beat the melted butter and erythritol together in a large bowl.*
3. *Add the eggs and almond extract and mix until the batter comes together.*
4. *Add the salt, baking powder and almond flour and mix until a nice, smooth batter forms.*
5. *Fold in the chopped almonds then scoop the cookie dough onto the prepared sheet tray. You will want to leave about 2 inches between the cookie dough scoops as the dough will spread slightly. If needed, you can bake the cookies in batches.*
6. *Bake the cookies in the air fryer for 8-9 minutes or until golden brown on the edges.*
7. *Let cool on the sheet tray for 5 minutes before removing and enjoying!*

NUTRITION: *Calories 176, Total Fat 24g, Saturated Fat 6g, Total Carbs 4g, Net Carbs 1g, Protein 6g, Sugar 1g, Fiber 3g, Sodium 348mg, Potassium 311g*

176. Chocolate Chip Almond Cookies

Preparation time: 10 minutes

Cooking time: 9 minutes Servings: 12

INGREDIENTS

- *½ cup butter, melted*
- *¾ cup erythritol*
- *1 tsp almond extract 1 egg*
- *1 ½ cups almond flour*
- *½ tsp salt*
- *½ tsp baking powder*
- *½ cup sugar free chocolate chips*
- *¼ cup sliced almonds*

DIRECTIONS

1. *Preheat your air fryer to 330 degrees F and prepare your air fryer tray with a piece of parchment.*
2. *Beat the melted butter and erythritol together in a large bowl.*
3. *Add the eggs and almond extract and mix until the batter comes together.*
4. *Add the salt, baking powder and almond flour and mix until a nice, smooth batter forms.*
5. *Fold in the sliced almonds then scoop the cookie dough onto the prepared sheet tray. You will want to leave about 2 inches between the cookie dough scoops as the dough will spread slightly. If needed, you can bake the cookies in batches.*
6. *Bake the cookies in the air fryer for 8-9 minutes or until golden brown on the edges.*
7. *Let cool on the sheet tray for 5 minutes before removing and enjoying!*

NUTRITION: *Calories 174, Total Fat 19g, Saturated Fat 7g, Total Carbs 3g, Net Carbs 1g, Protein 5g, Sugar 1g, Fiber 2g, Sodium 342mg, Potassium 281g*

177. Peanut Butter Cookies

Preparation time: 10 minutes

Cooking time: 9 minutes Servings: 12

INGREDIENTS

- *¼ cup butter, melted*
- *½ cup peanut butter*
- *¾ cup erythritol*
- *1 tsp vanilla extract 1 egg*
- *1 ½ cups almond flour*
- *½ tsp salt*
- *½ tsp baking powder*

DIRECTIONS

1. *Preheat your air fryer to 330 degrees F and prepare your air fryer tray with a piece of parchment.*
2. *Beat the melted butter, peanut butter and erythritol together in a large bowl.*
3. *Add the eggs and vanilla and mix until the batter comes together.*
4. *Add the salt, baking powder and almond flour and mix until a nice, smooth batter forms.*
5. *Scoop the cookie dough onto the prepared sheet tray. You will want to leave about 2 inches between the cookie dough scoops as the dough will spread slightly. If needed, you can bake the cookies in batches.*
6. *Bake the cookies in the air fryer for 8-9 minutes or until golden brown on the edges.*
7. *Let cool on the sheet tray for 5 minutes before removing and enjoying!*

NUTRITION: *Calories 189, Total Fat 24g, Saturated Fat 8g, Total Carbs 4g, Net Carbs 2g, Protein 6g, Sugar 2g, Fiber 2g, Sodium 354mg, Potassium 199g*

178. Peanut Butter Chocolate Chip Cookies

Preparation time: 10 minutes

Cooking time: 9 minutes Servings: 12

INGREDIENTS

- *¼ cup butter, melted*
- *½ cup peanut butter*
- *¾ cup erythritol*
- *1 tsp vanilla extract 1 egg*
- *1 ½ cups almond flour*
- *½ tsp salt*
- *½ tsp baking powder*
- *¾ cup sugar free chocolate chips*

DIRECTIONS

1. *Preheat your air fryer to 330 degrees F and prepare your air fryer tray with a piece of parchment.*
2. *Beat the melted butter, peanut butter and erythritol together in a large bowl.*
3. *Add the eggs and vanilla and mix until the batter comes together.*
4. *Add the salt, baking powder and almond flour and mix until a nice, smooth batter*

forms.

5. *Fold in the chocolate chips then scoop the cookie dough onto the prepared sheet tray. You will want to leave about 2 inches between the cookie dough scoops as the dough will spread slightly. If needed, you can bake the cookies in batches.*
6. *Bake the cookies in the air fryer for 8-9 minutes or until golden brown on the edges.*
7. *Let cool on the sheet tray for 5 minutes before removing and enjoying!*

NUTRITION: *Calories 219, Total Fat 26g, Saturated Fat 9g, Total Carbs 5g, Net Carbs 2g, Protein 6g, Sugar 1g, Fiber 3g, Sodium 354mg, Potassium 199g*

179. Hazelnut Cookies

Preparation time: 10 minutes

Cooking time: 9 minutes Servings: 12

INGREDIENTS

- *½ cup butter, melted*
- *¾ cup erythritol*
- *1 tsp vanilla extract 1 egg*
- *1 ½ cups hazelnut flour*
- *½ tsp salt*
- *½ tsp baking powder*

DIRECTIONS

1. *Preheat your air fryer to 330 degrees F and prepare your air fryer tray with a piece of parchment.*
2. *Beat the melted butter and erythritol together in a large bowl.*
3. *Add the eggs and vanilla and mix until the batter comes together.*
4. *Add the salt, baking powder and hazelnut flour and mix until a nice, smooth batter forms.*
5. *Scoop the cookie dough onto the prepared sheet tray. You will want to leave about 2 inches between the cookie dough scoops as the dough will spread slightly. If needed, you can bake the cookies in batches.*
6. *Bake the cookies in the air fryer for 8-9 minutes or until golden brown on the edges.*
7. *Let cool on the sheet tray for 5 minutes*

   before removing and enjoying!

NUTRITION: *Calories 134, Total Fat 11g, Saturated Fat 4g, Total Carbs 1g, Net Carbs 0g, Protein 4g, Sugar 0g, Fiber 1g, Sodium 342mg, Potassium 110g*

180. Hazelnut Chocolate Chip Cookies

Preparation time: 10 minutes

Cooking time: 9 minutes Servings: 12

INGREDIENTS

- *½ cup butter, melted*
- *¾ cup erythritol*
- *1 tsp vanilla extract 1 egg*
- *1 ½ cups hazelnut flour*
- *½ tsp salt*
- *½ tsp baking powder*
- *¾ cup sugar free chocolate chips*

DIRECTIONS

1. *Preheat your air fryer to 330 degrees F and prepare your air fryer tray with a piece of parchment.*
2. *Beat the melted butter and erythritol together in a large bowl.*
3. *Add the eggs and vanilla and mix until the batter comes together.*
4. *Add the salt, baking powder and hazelnut flour and mix until a nice, smooth batter forms.*
5. *Fold in the chocolate chips then scoop the cookie dough onto the prepared sheet tray. You will want to leave about 2 inches between the cookie dough scoops as the dough will spread slightly. If needed, you can bake the cookies in batches.*
6. *Bake the cookies in the air fryer for 8-9 minutes or until golden brown on the edges.*
7. *Let cool on the sheet tray for 5 minutes before removing and enjoying!*

NUTRITION: *Calories 173, Total Fat 18g, Saturated Fat 6g, Total Carbs 2g, Net Carbs 1g, Protein 5g, Sugar 1g, Fiber 3g, Sodium 342mg, Potassium 110g*

181. Seedy Cookies

Preparation time: 10 minutes

Cooking time: 9 minutes Servings: 12

INGREDIENTS

- *½ cup butter, melted*
- *¾ cup erythritol*
- *1 tsp vanilla extract 1 egg*
- *1 ½ cups almond flour*
- *½ tsp salt*
- *½ tsp baking powder*
- *¼ cup chia seeds*
- *¼ cup hemp seeds*
- *¼ cup sesame seeds*

DIRECTIONS

1. *Preheat your air fryer to 330 degrees F and prepare your air fryer tray with a piece of parchment.*
2. *Beat the melted butter and erythritol together in a large bowl.*
3. *Add the eggs and vanilla and mix until the batter comes together.*
4. *Add the salt, baking powder and almond flour and mix until a nice, smooth batter forms.*
5. *Fold in all the seeds then scoop the cookie dough onto the prepared sheet tray. You will want to leave about 2 inches between the cookie dough scoops as the dough will spread slightly. If needed, you can bake the cookies in batches.*
6. *Bake the cookies in the air fryer for 8-9 minutes or until golden brown on the edges.*
7. *Let cool on the sheet tray for 5 minutes before removing and enjoying!*

NUTRITION: *Calories 197, Total Fat 21g, Saturated Fat 5g, Total Carbs 7g, Net Carbs 4g, Protein 9g, Sugar 1g, Fiber 3g, Sodium 342mg, Potassium 188g*

182. Raspberry Cookies

Preparation time: 10 minutes

Cooking time: 9 minutes Servings: 12

INGREDIENTS

- *½ cup butter, melted*
- *¾ cup erythritol*
- *1 tsp vanilla extract 1 egg*
- *1 ½ cups almond flour*
- *½ tsp salt*
- *½ tsp baking powder*
- *½ cup fresh raspberries*

DIRECTIONS

1. *Preheat your air fryer to 330 degrees F and prepare your air fryer tray with a piece of parchment.*
2. *Beat the melted butter and erythritol together in a large bowl.*
3. *Add the eggs and vanilla and mix until the batter comes together.*
4. *Add the salt, baking powder and almond flour and mix until a nice, smooth batter forms.*
5. *Fold in the raspberries, smashing them slightly into the dough, then scoop the cookie dough onto the prepared sheet tray. You will want to leave about 2*
6. *inches between the cookie dough scoops as the dough will spread slightly. If needed, you can bake the cookies in batches.*
7. *Bake the cookies in the air fryer for 8-9 minutes or until golden brown on the edges.*
8. *Let cool on the sheet tray for 5 minutes before removing and enjoying!*

NUTRITION: *Calories 152, Total Fat 16g, Saturated Fat 4g, Total Carbs 7g, Net Carbs 4g, Protein 4g, Sugar 3g, Fiber 3g, Sodium 288mg, Potassium 67g*

183. Cocoa Cookies

Preparation time: 10 minutes

Cooking time: 9 minutes Servings: 12

INGREDIENTS

- *½ cup butter, melted*
- *¾ cup erythritol*
- *1 tsp vanilla extract 1 egg*
- *1 ¼ cups almond flour*
- *¼ cup cocoa powder*
- *½ tsp salt*
- *½ tsp baking powder*

DIRECTIONS

1. *Preheat your air fryer to 330 degrees F and prepare your air fryer tray with a piece of parchment.*
2. *Beat the melted butter and erythritol together in a large bowl.*
3. *Add the eggs and vanilla and mix until the batter comes together.*
4. *Add the salt, baking powder, cocoa powder and almond flour and mix until a nice, smooth batter forms.*
5. *Scoop the cookie dough onto the prepared sheet tray. You will want to leave about 2 inches between the cookie dough scoops as the dough will spread slightly. If needed, you can bake the cookies in batches.*
6. *Bake the cookies in the air fryer for 8-9 minutes or until golden brown on the edges.*
7. *Let cool on the sheet tray for 5 minutes before removing and enjoying!*

NUTRITION: *Calories 156, Total Fat 19g, Saturated Fat 7g, Total Carbs 2g, Net Carbs 1g, Protein 4g, Sugar 1g, Fiber 3g, Sodium 310mg, Potassium 101g*

184. Double Chocolate Cookies

Preparation time: 10 minutes

Cooking time: 9 minutes
Servings: 12

INGREDIENTS

- *½ cup butter, melted*
- *¾ cup erythritol*
- *1 tsp vanilla extract 1 egg*
- *1 ¼ cups almond flour*
- *¼ cup cocoa powder*
- *½ tsp salt*
- *½ tsp baking powder*
- *¾ cup unsweetened chocolate chips*

DIRECTIONS

1. *Preheat your air fryer to 330 degrees F and prepare your air fryer tray with a piece of parchment.*
2. *Beat the melted butter and erythritol together in a large bowl.*
3. *Add the eggs and vanilla and mix until the batter comes together.*
4. *Add the salt, baking powder, cocoa powder and almond flour and mix until a nice, smooth batter forms.*
5. *Fold in the chocolate chips then scoop the cookie dough onto the prepared sheet tray. You will want to leave about 2*

   inches between the cookie dough scoops as the dough will spread slightly. If needed, you can bake the cookies in batches.
6. *Bake the cookies in the air fryer for 8-9 minutes or until golden brown on the edges.*
7. *Let cool on the sheet tray for 5 minutes before removing and enjoying!*

NUTRITION: *Calories 188, Total Fat 21g, Saturated Fat 7g, Total Carbs 2g, Net Carbs 1g, Protein 5g, Sugar 1g, Fiber 3g, Sodium 311mg, Potassium 132g*

185. Peanut Butter Chocolate Cookies

Preparation time: 10 minutes

Cooking time: 9 minutes Servings: 12

INGREDIENTS

- *¼ cup butter, melted*
- *¼ cup peanut butter*
- *¾ cup erythritol*
- *1 tsp vanilla extract 1 egg*
- *1 ¼ cups almond flour*
- *¼ cup cocoa powder*
- *½ tsp salt*
- *½ tsp baking powder*

DIRECTIONS

1. *Preheat your air fryer to 330 degrees F and prepare your air fryer tray with a piece of parchment.*
2. *Beat the melted butter, peanut butter and erythritol together in a large bowl.*
3. *Add the eggs and vanilla and mix until the batter comes together.*
4. *Add the salt, baking powder, cocoa powder and almond flour and mix until a nice, smooth batter forms.*
5. *Scoop the cookie dough onto the prepared sheet tray. You will want to leave about 2 inches between the cookie dough scoops as the dough will spread slightly. If needed, you can bake the cookies in batches.*
6. *Bake the cookies in the air fryer for 8-9 minutes or until golden brown on the edges.*
7. *Let cool on the sheet tray for 5 minutes before removing and enjoying!*

NUTRITION: *Calories 172, Total Fat 22g, Saturated Fat 9g, Total Carbs 5g, Net Carbs 3g, Protein 6g, Sugar 1g, Fiber 2g, Sodium 310mg, Potassium 101g*

186. Cinnamon Chocolate Chip Cookies

Preparation time: 10 minutes

Cooking time: 9 minutes Servings: 12

INGREDIENTS

- *½ cup butter, melted*
- *¾ cup erythritol*
- *1 tsp vanilla extract 1 egg*
- *1 ½ cups almond flour 1 tsp ground cinnamon*
- *½ tsp salt*
- *½ tsp baking powder*
- *¾ cup sugar free chocolate chips*

DIRECTIONS

1. *Preheat your air fryer to 330 degrees F and prepare your air fryer tray with a piece of parchment.*
2. *Beat the melted butter and erythritol together in a large bowl.*
3. *Add the eggs and vanilla and mix until the batter comes together.*
4. *Add the salt, baking powder, cinnamon and almond flour and mix until a nice, smooth batter forms.*
5. *Fold in the chocolate chips then scoop the cookie dough onto the prepared sheet tray. You will want to leave about 2 inches between the cookie dough scoops as the dough will spread slightly. If needed, you can bake the cookies in batches.*
6. *Bake the cookies in the air fryer for 8-9 minutes or until golden brown on the edges.*
7. *Let cool on the sheet tray for 5 minutes before removing and enjoying!*

NUTRITION: *Calories 169, Total Fat 19g, Saturated Fat 7g, Total Carbs 2g, Net Carbs 1g, Protein 4g, Sugar 1g, Fiber 1g, Sodium 342mg, Potassium 110g*

187. Pumpkin Spice Cookies

Preparation time: 10 minutes

Cooking time: 9 minutes

Servings: 12

INGREDIENTS

- *¼ cup butter, melted*
- *¼ cup pumpkin puree*
- *¾ cup erythritol*
- *1 tsp vanilla extract 1 egg*
- *1 ½ cups almond flour*
- *½ tsp salt*
- *1 tsp pumpkin spice seasoning*
- *½ tsp baking powder*

DIRECTIONS

1. *Preheat your air fryer to 330 degrees F and prepare your air fryer tray with a piece of parchment.*
2. *Beat the melted butter, pumpkin puree and erythritol together in a large bowl.*
3. *Add the eggs and vanilla and mix until the batter comes together.*
4. *Add the salt, baking powder, pumpkin spice seasoning and almond flour and mix until a nice, smooth batter forms.*
5. *Scoop the cookie dough onto the prepared sheet tray. You will want to leave about 2 inches between the cookie dough scoops as the dough will spread slightly. If needed, you can bake the cookies in batches.*
6. *Bake the cookies in the air fryer for 8-9 minutes or until golden brown on the edges.*
7. *Let cool on the sheet tray for 5 minutes before removing and enjoying!*

NUTRITION: *Calories 188, Total Fat 16g, Saturated Fat 5g, Total Carbs 7g, Net Carbs 3g, Protein 4g, Sugar 2g, Fiber 4g, Sodium 482mg, Potassium 346g*

188. Pumpkin Chocolate Chip Cookies

Preparation time: 10 minutes

Cooking time: 9 minutes
Servings: 12

INGREDIENTS

- *¼ cup butter, melted*
- *¼ cup pumpkin puree*
- *¾ cup erythritol*
- *1 tsp vanilla extract 1 egg*
- *1 ½ cups almond flour*
- *½ tsp salt*
- *1 tsp pumpkin spice seasoning*
- *½ tsp baking powder*
- *¾ cup sugar free chocolate chips*

DIRECTIONS

1. *Preheat your air fryer to 330 degrees F and prepare your air fryer tray with a piece of parchment.*
2. *Beat the melted butter, pumpkin puree and erythritol together in a large bowl.*
3. *Add the eggs and vanilla and mix until the batter comes together.*
4. *Add the salt, baking powder, pumpkin spice seasoning and almond flour and mix until a nice, smooth batter forms.*
5. *Fold in the chocolate chips then scoop the cookie dough onto the prepared sheet tray. You will want to leave about 2 inches between the cookie dough scoops as the dough will spread slightly. If needed, you can bake the cookies in batches.*
6. *Bake the cookies in the air fryer for 8-9 minutes or until golden brown on the edges.*
7. *Let cool on the sheet tray for 5 minutes before removing and enjoying!*

NUTRITION: *Calories 218, Total Fat 27g, Saturated Fat 8g, Total Carbs 7g, Net Carbs 3g, Protein 4g, Sugar 2g, Fiber 4g, Sodium 482mg, Potassium 346g*

189. Cream Cheese Cookies

Preparation time: 10 minutes

Cooking time: 9 minutes Servings: 12

INGREDIENTS

- *½ cup cream cheese, softened*
- *¾ cup erythritol*
- *1 tsp vanilla extract 1 egg*
- *1 ½ cups almond flour*
- *½ tsp salt*
- *½ tsp baking powder*

DIRECTIONS

1. *Preheat your air fryer to 330 degrees F and prepare your air fryer tray with a piece of parchment.*
2. *Beat the cream cheese and erythritol together in a large bowl.*
3. *Add the eggs and vanilla and mix until the batter comes together.*
4. *Add the salt, baking powder, pumpkin spice seasoning and almond flour and mix until a nice, smooth batter forms.*
5. *Scoop the cookie dough onto the prepared sheet tray. You will want to leave about 2 inches between the cookie dough scoops as the dough will spread slightly. If needed, you can bake the cookies in batches.*
6. *Bake the cookies in the air fryer for 8-9 minutes or until golden brown on the edges.*
7. *Let cool on the sheet tray for 5 minutes before removing and enjoying!*

NUTRITION: *Calories 189, Total Fat 11g, Saturated Fat 6g, Total Carbs 2g, Net Carbs 1g, Protein 4g, Sugar 1g, Fiber 1g, Sodium 211 mg, Potassium 101g*

190. Keto Shortbread

Preparation time: 15 minutes

Cooking time: 15 minutes Servings: 8

INGREDIENTS

- *½ cup butter*
- *½ cup swerve sweetener 1 tsp vanilla extract*
- *1 cup almond flour 1 tsp salt*

DIRECTIONS

1. *Preheat your air fryer to 300 degrees F and grease a 6 inch baking pan or tray.*
2. *Place the butter and swerve sweetener in a mixing bowl and beat until soft and fluffy.*
3. *Add the vanilla extract and beat again to incorporate fully.*
4. *Add the almond flour slowly, mixing it in a little at a time, until a smooth dough has formed.*
5. *Spread the shortbread batter in the prepared baking pan or tray and then place in the preheated air fryer.*
6. *Bake for 15 minutes or until the edges of the shortbread are golden brown.*
7. *Let cool for 10 minutes then flip the shortbread out of the pan, slice and enjoy while warm.*

NUTRITION: *Calories 182, Total Fat 18g, Saturated Fat 7g, Total Carbs 3g, Net Carbs 2g,*

Protein 3g, Sugar 1g, Fiber 1g, Sodium 364mg, Potassium 78g

191. Lemon Shortbread

Preparation time: 15 minutes

Cooking time: 15 minutes Servings: 8

INGREDIENTS

- *½ cup butter*
- *½ cup swerve sweetener 1 tsp vanilla extract*
- *1 cup almond flour 1 tsp salt*
- *1 tsp lemon zest*

DIRECTIONS

1. *Preheat your air fryer to 300 degrees F and grease a 6 inch baking pan or tray.*
2. *Place the butter and swerve sweetener in a mixing bowl and beat until soft and fluffy.*
3. *Add the vanilla extract and lemon zest and beat again to incorporate fully.*
4. *Add the almond flour slowly, mixing it in a little at a time, until a smooth dough has formed.*
5. *Spread the shortbread batter in the prepared baking pan or tray and then place in the preheated air fryer.*
6. *Bake for 15 minutes or until the edges of the shortbread are golden brown.*
7. *Let cool for 10 minutes then flip the shortbread out of the pan, slice and enjoy while warm.*

NUTRITION: *Calories 189, Total Fat 19g, Saturated Fat 7g, Total Carbs 3g, Net Carbs 2g, Protein 3g, Sugar 1g, Fiber 1g, Sodium 364mg, Potassium 78g*

192. Almond Shortbread

Preparation time: 15 minutes

Cooking time: 15 minutes Servings: 8

INGREDIENTS

- *½ cup butter*
- *½ cup swerve sweetener 1 tsp almond extract*
- *1 cup almond flour*
- *1 tsp salt*
- *½ cup sliced almonds*

DIRECTIONS

1. *Preheat your air fryer to 300 degrees F*

   and grease a 6 inch baking pan or tray.
2. *Place the butter and swerve sweetener in a mixing bowl and beat until soft and fluffy.*
3. *Add the almond extract and beat again to incorporate fully.*
4. *Add the almond flour slowly, mixing it in a little at a time, until a smooth dough has formed.*
5. *Spread the shortbread batter in the prepared baking pan or tray and then sprinkle the sliced almonds over the top of the shortbread.*
6. *Place in the preheated air fryer and bake for*
7. *15 minutes or until the edges of the shortbread are golden brown.*
8. *Let cool for 10 minutes then flip the shortbread out of the pan, slice and enjoy while warm.*

NUTRITION: *Calories 216, Total Fat 24g, Saturated Fat 9g, Total Carbs 3g, Net Carbs 2g, Protein 3g, Sugar 1g, Fiber 1g, Sodium 364mg, Potassium 78g*

193. Lime Shortbread

Preparation time: 15 minutes

Cooking time: 15 minutes Servings: 8

INGREDIENTS

- *½ cup butter*
- *½ cup swerve sweetener 1 tsp vanilla extract*
- *1 cup almond flour 1 tsp salt*
- *1 tsp lime zest*

DIRECTIONS

1. *Preheat your air fryer to 300 degrees F and grease a 6 inch baking pan or tray.*
2. *Place the butter and swerve sweetener in a mixing bowl and beat until soft and fluffy.*
3. *Add the vanilla extract and lime zest and beat again to incorporate fully.*
4. *Add the almond flour slowly, mixing it in a little at a time, until a smooth dough has formed.*
5. *Spread the shortbread batter in the prepared baking pan or tray and then place in the preheated air fryer.*
6. *Bake for 15 minutes or until the edges of*

the shortbread are golden brown.

7. *Let cool for 10 minutes then flip the shortbread out of the pan, slice and enjoy while warm.*

NUTRITION: *Calories 184, Total Fat 18g, Saturated Fat 7g, Total Carbs 3g, Net Carbs 2g, Protein 3g, Sugar 1g, Fiber 1g, Sodium 364mg, Potassium 78g*

194. Chocolate Shortbread

Preparation time: 15 minutes

Cooking time: 15 minutes
Servings: 8

INGREDIENTS

- *½ cup butter*
- *½ cup swerve sweetener 1 tsp vanilla extract*
- *¾ cup almond flour*
- *¼ cup cocoa powder 1 tsp salt*

DIRECTIONS

1. *Preheat your air fryer to 300 degrees F and grease a 6 inch baking pan or tray.*
2. *Place the butter and swerve sweetener in a mixing bowl and beat until soft and fluffy.*
3. *Add the vanilla extract and beat again to incorporate fully.*
4. *Add the almond flour and cocoa powder slowly, mixing them in a little at a time, until a smooth dough has formed.*
5. *Spread the shortbread batter in the prepared baking pan or tray and then place in the preheated air fryer.*
6. *Bake for 15 minutes or until the edges of the shortbread are golden brown.*
7. *Let cool for 10 minutes then flip the shortbread out of the pan, slice and enjoy while warm.*

NUTRITION: *Calories 204, Total Fat 20g, Saturated Fat 7g, Total Carbs 3g, Net Carbs 2g, Protein 4g, Sugar 1g, Fiber 1g, Sodium 364mg, Potassium 89g*

195. Chocolate Chip Shortbread

Preparation time: 15 minutes

Cooking time: 15 minutes Servings: 8

INGREDIENTS

- *½ cup butter*
- *½ cup swerve sweetener 1 tsp vanilla extract*
- *1 cup almond flour 1 tsp salt*
- *½ cup dark chocolate chips, unsweetened*

DIRECTIONS

1. *Preheat your air fryer to 300 degrees F and grease a 6 inch baking pan or tray.*
2. *Place the butter and swerve sweetener in a mixing bowl and beat until soft and fluffy.*
3. *Add the vanilla extract and beat again to incorporate fully.*
4. *Add the almond flour slowly, mixing it in a little at a time, until a smooth dough has formed.*
5. *Fold in the chocolate chips gently.*
6. *Spread the shortbread batter in the prepared baking pan or tray and then place in the preheated air fryer.*
7. *Bake for 15 minutes or until the edges of the shortbread are golden brown.*
8. *Let cool for 10 minutes then flip the shortbread out of the pan, slice and enjoy while warm.*

NUTRITION: *Calories 230, Total Fat 23g, Saturated Fat 9g, Total Carbs 4g, Net Carbs 2g, Protein 6g, Sugar 1g, Fiber 2g, Sodium 364mg, Potassium 78g*

196. 873. Peanut Butter Shortbread

Preparation time: 15 minutes

Cooking time: 15 minutes

Servings: 8

INGREDIENTS

- *½ cup peanut butter*
- *½ cup swerve sweetener 1 tsp vanilla extract*
- *1 cup almond flour 1 tsp salt*

DIRECTIONS

1. *Preheat your air fryer to 300 degrees F and grease a 6 inch baking pan or tray.*
2. *Place the peanut butter and swerve sweetener in a mixing bowl and beat until soft and fluffy.*
3. *Add the vanilla extract and beat again to incorporate fully.*
4. *Add the almond flour slowly, mixing it in a little at a time, until a smooth dough has formed.*
5. *Spread the shortbread batter in the prepared baking pan or tray and then place in the preheated air fryer.*
6. *Bake for 15 minutes or until the edges of the shortbread are golden brown.*
7. *Let cool for 10 minutes then flip the shortbread out of the pan, slice and enjoy while warm.*

NUTRITION: *Calories 189, Total Fat 19g, Saturated Fat 7g, Total Carbs 5g, Net Carbs 4g, Protein 3g, Sugar 2g, Fiber 1g, Sodium 364mg, Potassium 78g*

197. Walnut Shortbread

Preparation time: 15 minutes

Cooking time: 15 minutes Servings: 8

INGREDIENTS

- *½ cup butter*
- *½ cup swerve sweetener 1 tsp vanilla extract*
- *1 cup walnut flour 1 tsp salt*

DIRECTIONS

1. *Preheat your air fryer to 300 degrees F and grease a 6 inch baking pan or tray.*
2. *Place the butter and swerve sweetener in a mixing bowl and beat until soft and fluffy.*
3. *Add the vanilla extract and beat again to incorporate fully.*
4. *Add the walnut flour slowly, mixing it in a little at a time, until a smooth dough has formed.*
5. *Spread the shortbread batter in the prepared baking pan or tray and then place in the preheated air fryer.*
6. *Bake for 15 minutes or until the edges of the shortbread are golden brown.*
7. *Let cool for 10 minutes then flip the shortbread out of the pan, slice and enjoy while warm.*

NUTRITION: *Calories 188, Total Fat 18g, Saturated Fat 7g, Total Carbs 3g, Net Carbs 2g, Protein 3g, Sugar 1g, Fiber 1g, Sodium 358mg, Potassium 76g*

198. Coconut Shortbread

Preparation time: 15 minutes

Cooking time: 15 minutes Servings: 8

INGREDIENTS

- *½ cup butter*
- *½ cup swerve sweetener 1 tsp coconut extract*
- *½ cup almond flour*
- *½ cup coconut flour 1 tsp salt*

DIRECTIONS

1. *Preheat your air fryer to 300 degrees F and grease a 6 inch baking pan or tray.*
2. *Place the butter and swerve sweetener in a mixing bowl and beat until soft and fluffy.*
3. *Add the coconut extract and beat again to incorporate fully.*
4. *Add the almond flour and coconut flour slowly, mixing them in a little at a time, until a smooth dough has formed.*
5. *Spread the shortbread batter in the prepared baking pan or tray and then place in the preheated air fryer.*
6. *Bake for 15 minutes or until the edges of the shortbread are golden brown.*
7. *Let cool for 10 minutes then flip the shortbread out of the pan, slice and enjoy while warm.*

NUTRITION: *Calories 196, Total Fat 20g, Saturated Fat 8g, Total Carbs 5g, Net Carbs 4g, Protein 3g, Sugar 3g, Fiber 1g, Sodium 364mg, Potassium 101g*

199. Peas with Bacon

Preparation time: 10 – 20 minutes
Cooking time: 30 – 45 minutes
Servings: 8

INGREDIENTS

- *750g of frozen peas 100g smoked bacon 2 shallots*
- *Salt and pepper to taste 200ml broth*

DIRECTION:

1. *Preheat the air fryer to 1600C for 5 minutes.*
2. *Pour the chopped onion, bacon, oil in the basket*
3. *Brown for 5 min.*
4. *Add the peas, broth, salt, pepper, and simmer for additional 30 minutes.*

NUTRITION: *Calories 129.6 Fat 6.0 g Carbohydrate 13.6g Sugars3.3g Protein6.0g Cholesterol7.7 mg*

200. Fresh Pizza

Preparation time: 10-20 minutes

Cooking time: 30-45 minutes Servings: 1

INGREDIENTS

- *70ml of water 125 g flour*
- *3g salt*
- *g fresh yeast 100 g of tomato 100 g mozzarella Oregano to taste*

DIRECTION:

1. *Pour the flour into a bowl, form a well, and then add the other ingredients in the center.*
2. *Knead with your hands until you get soft and flexible dough. Form a ball with this dough, and then let it grow in a previously floured bowl.*
3. *Cover with a clean cloth and let stand at room temperature, away from drafts. After about 1 hour of lifting, start spreading the dough*
4. *Preheat the air fryer to 1500C for 5 minutes.*
5. *Grease the bottom and spread the pizza dough. Cover with tomato coulis. Add a pinch of salt and oregano.*
6. *After 15 minutes cook add the diced mozzarella*
7. *Approximately after 10 minutes, turn the pizza half a turn*
8. *Cook for an additional 7 minutes.* NUTRITION: *Calories 290 Carbohydrates 36g Fat 11g Sugars 0g Protein 11g Cholesterol 15mg*

CONCLUSION

The air fryers have gained a lot of popularity over the last years due to their many advantages. Cooking in an air fryer is such a great and fun experience and you should try it as soon as possible.

The air fryer is such an innovative appliance that allows you to cook some of the best, most succulent and rich meals for you, your family and friends.

The air fryer reduces the cooking time and the effort you spend in the kitchen.

Get a copy of this amazing air fryer cooking guide and use it to make real feast using this great appliance. Start this culinary journey right away and enjoy the benefits of cooking with the air fryer.

CPSIA information can be obtained
at www.ICGtesting.com
Printed in the USA
LVHW061812310121
677957LV00008B/337

9 781801 596770